NED HALLEY is the *Family Circle* magazine wine correspondent and is also the wine writer for the Press Association. He has written more than 30 books, many on wine, but also best-selling children's titles and a number of guides to Britain. Born and educated in Scotland, he now lives in Somerset with his wife and two children.

D1638949

Absolute Corkers

A Wine Buff's Bedside Book of Anecdotes and Funny Stories

NED HALLEY

Illustrations by Paul Cox

CONSTABLE • LONDON

Constable & Robinson Ltd
3 The Lanchesters
162 Fulham Palace Road
London W6 9ER
www.constablerobinson.com

First published in the UK by Constable,
an imprint of Constable & Robinson Ltd, 2009

A copy of the British Library Cataloguing in
Publication data is available from the British Library

ISBN: 978-1-84529-853-1

Printed and bound in the EU

1 3 5 7 9 10 8 6 4 2

For Sheila, Max and Lydia

Contents

How to Become a Wine Writer   1

Best Stories of Winemakers and Great Wines   10

A Sniff of History   66

If You Really Want to Know   88

If You Ask My Advice   117

Bin Ends   151

The Last Drop   186

How to Become a Wine Writer

The real luminaries of the wine world are the dedicated growers of the grapes, and the alchemists of the cellars who effect the miraculous transformation of the harvest into the vintage. And let's not forget the men and women at the sharp end, the dealers and brokers, the importers and retailers who bring the finished product to market, in what has now become one of the most competitive – and overcrowded – businesses worldwide.

As a writer in this field since the 1980s, when the present wine boom was just getting under way, I have been able to visit winemakers and wine-sellers in all sorts of places. I have reported on thousands of wines – sniffed, slurped and sincerely deconstructed them, but I've not always told the stories of the delightful people and places behind them.

This has been remiss, because I have always considered myself a journalist first, and a wine writer second. In contrast to so many of my distinguished colleagues in the Circle of Wine Writers, who started out as wine professionals or cut their teeth in drinks-trade publications, I began my life in journalism as a general news reporter for an English-language daily paper in Hong Kong. I had some tricky assignments covering organized crime and exposing the countless shortcomings of the colonial government, but was also indulged by the editor with a larky opinion column, and the occasional restaurant review.

I had acquired a precocious interest in food and drink thanks to my grandparents. Home life in Scotland for my sister and I had fallen apart in childhood when our mother died suddenly and our father remarried unwisely and in haste. Our grieving granny rescued us and on our holidays from boarding school spoiled us unstintingly at her vast house in Newcastle (where we spent too much time in the kitchens with the cook), or on travels to the most fashionable resorts. In time, we were allowed to try sips of wine. I took to it.

Back in Britain from the Far East in pursuit of my future wife Sheila, I settled in London, and after failing to persuade the *Daily Telegraph* to take me on, overreacted to the disappointment by joining *Mayfair*, the saucy men's magazine. This no doubt revealed the true extent of my frivolousness, because I never had so much fun in my life. Besides becoming the magazine's undisputed desk-tennis champion, I invented laughable names, cosy provincial lives and unlikely erotic preferences for the curvaceous cuties (mostly German glamour models) who graced our centrefolds, compiled a notorious jokes page, and even took charge of the agony column. I lasted a year, and then somehow managed to transfer to the British edition of *Reader's Digest* magazine – a considerable cultural leap. Next stop, the glossy magazine *Ideal Home* as deputy editor, where I first wrote about wine.

This was around 1980, still the era of Liebfraumilch and Mateus Rosé. But magazines for the aspiring householder, which *Ideal Home* most definitely was, had a mission to elevate the public taste in all sorts of respects. This included educating readers on the finer points of wine, even offering them mixed cases of mildly pretentious bottles for home delivery at what purported to be advantageous prices. I was given the task of approaching an approved list of well-known wine companies, choosing the selections and writing the gushing blurbs. Compared to interviewing the endless TV celebrities whose lovely homes appeared in our pages, it was a breeze.

The magazine did have a wine column, and when the incumbent writer retired (voluntarily, I hope), I took it over. Immediately my name appeared on the page, I began to receive invitations to wine tastings. The first I accepted was from a dentist in Wiltshire, who sent a witty postcard with a catalogue, illustrated by Quentin Blake, of the wines he sold, part-time, from his home-cum-shop in the little town of Mere. It all sounded picturesque, and full of potential for a colour piece in the magazine. I telephoned to make the arrangements, and this unusual entrepreneur, Robin Yapp, gave me travel instructions. Take the train to Gillingham in Dorset. Come out of the station, turn right and right again and follow the road to the address of the dental surgery. In the waiting room, he would meet me after he'd finished with his last patient of the morning.

Was this really how the provincial wine trade functioned? I needed to know. It was a day of warm sunshine in May when I made the great journey, my first, I am ashamed to say, into the rural West Country. The directions were spot on, the waiting room like any other. The dentist was a different matter. He was huge and bearded, brimming with sly jokes and indiscreetly talkative – a gift to any interviewer. It was a good story. He had read dentistry at Leeds University and in the vacations worked as a waiter in the Royal Hotel at Scarborough, there acquiring an interest in wine thanks to the sommelier, who had allowed him to sample the occasional leftovers from great vintages, apparently in hope of sexual favours. Young Robin had survived with his virtue intact, qualified and set up in practice here in Dorset. He had married twice, first a fellow dentist and then the local GP, Judith Bell. Now besides their practices, the couple had lately added a child of their own to the six they shared from their respective dissolved marriages, and were both also working hard on their fast-growing wine business. It was called Yapp Bros. in memory of Robin's brother, another doctor, who had died tragically young.

All this I learned on the short drive to Mere along a maze of sun-bright lanes aglow with the bloom of cow parsley. Yapp HQ turned out to be the family home along with a couple of cottages adapted into offices and a quaint shop, plus several warehouses and a 60-foot brick chimney. Converted from an industrial site that had long ago been a brewery, and latterly a dairy, all the buildings were arranged around a gated central courtyard festooned with geraniums and, in the middle, an ornamental fountain. It was a copy, Robin told me, of the one in the village square of Châteauneuf du Pape, a precise replica in all but one respect: thanks to a mix-up over measurements, the London stone carver who had recreated the masterpiece from a photograph had made the Yapp version rather bigger than the original.

Larger than life proved to be the theme here. I had known nothing of Yapp Bros. before hearing from its owner, but now discovered that the firm was already the leading importer of serious-quality wines from the Loire and Rhône valleys of France, the regions in which Yapp had specialized from the start, ten years earlier. I was shown over the place, tasted some of the wines, had an epic lunch to which a couple of restaurant customers had also been invited, and had my eyes opened. Yapp really was an NHS dentist, but he could have passed equally convincingly for a full-time wine merchant. I noticed, however, that unlike other merchants I had thus far encountered, when tasting wines with him he did not tell you what you ought to be thinking about them. He did not use flowery language. He was, however, wildly enthusiastic about his discoveries. He had started simply by turning up at the doors of the *vignerons*, asking in his rather middling French for a taste, and buying the ones he liked – if there were any for sale. When there were none, I suspect he turned on the charm.

I will always be grateful to Robin, because he animated the world of wine for me. Thirty years on, he and Judith are now retired and their two sons have the business, but I am still scribbling away. In the interim, I have made the acquaintance of scores of wine merchants from one-man shows to the moguls of the supermarkets, and have visited countless winemakers across Europe and further afield. I have been on press trips which have included diversions such as playing football for England (wine-writers' XI) against Hungary (winemakers' XI) with John Arlott doing the touchline commentary, and being whispered to by a sinister American official in Chile that he didn't believe I was a wine journalist, but a spy.

And I have drunk the wines at the fountainhead. I have sipped Bollinger at Bollinger, Mouton-Rothschild at Mouton-Rothschild, Taylors at Taylors. There's been grape-picking in Burgundy, Chianti, even England (it rained) and pressing, by foot, in the ancient *lagars* of the port country. There have been hundreds of articles in newspapers and magazines, a dozen books, even my own wine magazine *Spyglass*, which lasted a brief, but happy, six years before proving the rule that it is as easy to fail as an independent publisher as it is to do so as an independent maker, or seller, of wine.

Wine journalism works like this. The people who make and market wine give their products to the people who write and broadcast about wine, in the hope that favourable reports will follow. The producers send out samples to accredited wine journalists, and regularly extend invitations to visit the vineyards, often with all expenses paid. Large producers organize these samplings and visits by dealing with the journalists directly. Smaller producers are represented collectively by co-operatives, regional associations or quasi-official national bodies such as Wines of Australia or France's Sopexa, the Société pour l'Expansion des Produits Agricoles et Alimentaires.

Most wine journalists would be unable to function without the assistance of these organizations. To buy the thousands of wines sampled per year in search of those worth writing about would be ruinously expensive, and the cost of travel to the vineyards, especially those on the far side of the planet, likewise. And anyway, to get to meet the world's more interesting winemakers, you really need an invitation. You don't just drop in.

Of course there are exceptions. The handful of wine writers who prosper greatly by their work can afford to buy the wines they wish to taste, and to travel at their own expense. And their good opinion is so valued by the winemakers that they can call in any time. Their 'support' is also valued by the wine trade. Merchants who once relied on their own judgement to decide whether to buy the new vintage from this or that vineyard, especially at the most expensive end of the market, now like to cross-check their own tasting notes with those of certain independent critics.

Well, all right, with one independent critic. Robert Parker, the American wine guru, overshadows all his colleagues. He has his own magazine, the *Wine Advocate*, in which he publishes his judgements on the world's leading wines, vintage by vintage, and has sold millions of books repackaging the information and opinions accumulated along the way. Parker has his own scoring system for wines. The best get 100 points and the worst 50. It's distinctive, easy to follow. And closely followed it is, by many wine merchants, restaurateurs and individual wine collectors, in America and beyond. Anything at 90 or above must be good. Anything below ranges from OK downwards.

It would all be just a bit of fun if it were not for the fact that the prices fetched by individual wines can be substantially affected by the scores Parker – ably aided by other tasters in his *Wine Advocate* team – gives to them as they go on the market. So slavish are some followers that a high-scoring wine can go for twice the price the maker might usually expect to get for it.

Parker has made the reputations, and even the fortunes, of some wine producers and, if only by omission, has done nothing to advance the good names of some others. He is not universally admired in the wider world of wine, but is a great advocate of France. His compliments have been repaid with the award of the Légion d'Honneur, at Chévalier rank, in 1999, followed by elevation to an Officer of the Order, a very senior honour, in 2005. The Italian state has given him equivalent recognition through the award of its Order of Merit.

If he was once a maverick champion of the consumer's right to a decent bottle of wine, Parker now finds himself more of an establishment figure. Born in Maryland in 1947, he was a lawyer until converting his enthusiasm for wine into a career in his early thirties. He claims to have discovered wine during a student vacation when visiting his girlfriend at the University of Strasbourg in France's Alsace region. It seems a very sensible place in which to make a first acquaintance with wine, and it commends Parker that Patricia, the girlfriend in question, was to become his wife, and still is.

Robert Parker has been the subject of countless adoring profiles in the media, and biographies including the entertaining *The Emperor of Wine* by Elin McCoy (Ecco, 2005). There have been equal numbers of cruel asides from his colleagues among the wine journalists, usually gleefully quoting the hurt feelings of wine producers who have not found favour with the ubiquitous Parker nose. There have been famous disagreements with other critics, such as the dispute, much relished in the wine world, with Britain's Jancis Robinson. She is acknowledged as at least equal to Parker in expertise if not in influence, and differed with him over a renowned wine from St Emilion in Bordeaux, Chateau Pavie 2003. Parker loved it, Robinson hated it. The innocent bystander could have been forgiven for wondering if the two of them were even talking about the same wine.

When wine critics do disagree strongly about what is good and what is not, should we all laugh or cry? Laughter is the only recourse. Taste is personal in all things, and more so in wine than in just about anything else. And we are all as much at liberty to make our choices among the critics as we are among the wines themselves.

All that matters is that trust in the critics is reasonably consensual. If their motivation is beyond reproach, we can relax. For what it's worth, I have met Robert Parker, and liked him at once. It was long ago, when he was an opinion-holder rather than an opinion-former, but I have gleaned from his writings that he is still motivated by the honest desire to find and describe the best wines. I have met Jancis Robinson rather more often, and cannot fault her awesome but infectiously good-humoured authority.

As for the rest of us – in the several divisions of writers below the premier crew of Parker, Robinson and a very few others – I have come across plenty of out-and-out phoneys and freeloaders over the years, but these days detect a steady growth in analytical skills and old-fashioned enthusiasm. There are other less welcome characteristics common to newly aspiring wine writers too, including po-faced seriousness, political correctness and unreasoning bias in favour of 'New World' wines, but on balance, the trend away from the silly snobs of old is to be welcomed.

Not so long ago, many of the writers were also working in the wine trade (it's never been easy to make a living just writing about the product), and were naturally tempted to endorse the wines made by themselves, or their employers, or by their chums in the business. Today, more writers are independent without being any the less qualified. The Circle of Wine Writers, British-based but with members everywhere, asks all of them to make declarations about any trade interests, and acts as a kind of accreditation body.

As a writer, I have had a great deal of hospitality from the people who make and sell wine. Along with numerous colleagues, I am invited every year to scores of tastings, and a few press visits abroad, mostly in Europe, occasionally further afield.

Tastings are indispensable. I once worked out that if I had been obliged to buy a bottle each of the wines I had tasted during one year, the damage would have been about £50,000. And as to visiting some of the faraway vineyards to which I have kindly been flown – by private jet on more than one occasion – I wouldn't have missed it for the world. These organized trips are usually sociable and some-times seem, in retrospect, a bit pointless, but there is an argument that without seeing where and how the wines are actually made and meeting the people who do it all, you'd never really get a grip on the subject. I'm prepared to believe it.

Along the wine routes, I have found many memorable wines, some funny and happy experiences and unearthed some unusual stories and facts about wine. Some of them I have already shared willingly with readers of the newspapers and magazines I write for now, or have in the past. Others I have not been in such a hurry to make known. This is my chance.

Best Stories of
Winemakers and Great Wines

EXPERT OPINION

Dudley Quirk, who started making good English wine in the 1970s at his vineyard in Chiddingstone, Kent, was pleased when the Queen had it served at a Buckingham Palace banquet in honour of the President of France. Dudley knew very well the value of good publicity. He relished the leading article in *The Times* published on the occasion, and enjoyed showing TV crews over his vines and winery, usually in pouring rain.

But he was wary of the 'expert' wine writers who would come to visit and give him lofty advice on viticulture, winery practice, the market and so on. This was largely because he was making a most unusual kind of English wine, dry and mineral in the Loire Valley style rather than the sugared, flabby Liebfraumilch-style stuff then preferred by English producers – and loyally praised in all sorts of flowery, pseudo-scientific language by the trade press. When I went to interview Dudley for a glossy magazine and it was quickly established that I was a dilettante of wine at best, he confided to me his opinion of my more serious-minded colleagues.

'An expert, as far as I am concerned,' he said, 'is somebody who is away from home.'

LAUGHTER AT LAFITE

I once stayed for a few days at Château Lafite. Baron Eric de Rothschild, whose family business owns the estate, is a kind and entertaining host, and proud to show off the place, and its wines, to hacks like me.

On my visit, as one of a group of half a dozen writers, I was very courteously shown to my room in the beautiful house by the Baron in person. This handsome scion of Europe's premier banking dynasty informed me, not without relish, that the baroque Empire bed I would be sleeping in was the one in which his great-great grandfather, Baron James de Rothschild, who bought Lafite in 1868, had breathed his last.

Baron Eric apologized that all the guest rooms with their own bathrooms were to be occupied by the ladies among our party. But he offered consolation as he opened the door to a *lavabo* recessed into the room's eighteenth-century panelling. 'As you are English,' he told me jauntily, 'you will no doubt make use of this if you need to piddle in the night.'

He hooted with laughter at this indelicacy, and I did like him for it. In the ensuing days, in which he guided our little group around Lafite and several other properties also owned by the family, there was a great deal more laughter.

On one evening, sitting next to Baron Eric's wife at dinner, I discovered she was a vegetarian. While the rest of us were eating Pauillac lamb – very much a local speciality – she was toying with some sort of salad. Aware of the rivalry that exists between nearby Château Mouton-Rothschild, owned by a separate branch of the family, and Lafite, I idiotically pointed to la Baronne's leafy repast and said to her, '*Aha, pas de* Mouton *ici!*'

The moment I said it I regretted it, and prayed she would ignore the remark. Instead, she grasped my arm and dissolved into peals of laughter. Worse was to come. To my horror, she now called across the great circular table to her husband opposite and repeated the saga to him, and so to the entire company.

Rothschild made out that he thought it every bit as funny as his wife did, and for the remainder of our visit, he missed few opportunities to remind me of it. '*Pas de* Mouton,' he would mutter, shaking his head.

I learned much from my visit to Lafite. Most of all I learned that it's possible to make the best wine in the world without taking it all too seriously.

WORLD'S RICHEST FARMLAND

The four-and-a-half acre vineyard of La Romanée Conti was first identified in 1232 on purchase by the Abbey of St Vivant, in what is now the village of Vosne-Romanée, just north of Nuits-St-Georges in Burgundy. The same plot, known as a *monopole*, because it is owned exclusively by one company, the Domaine de la Romanée Conti (DRC), is now the most financially productive farmland in the world. From a few rows of Pinot Noir vines with an average age of more than 50 years, the DRC makes about 5,500 bottles of wine per harvest. Prices vary with the vintage, but £5,000 per bottle is typical enough for in-demand new releases. This means the DRC can gross about £500,000 per acre in a good year. Cereal farmers in France, or anywhere else, would consider it a miracle to get within any distance of £500 per acre.

La Romanée Conti is an unremarkable stretch of land, quite flat, but with a nice low stone wall around it. On the day I visited recently, there was a young man hoeing between the vines with the aid of a horse. Why go to the expense of a tractor?

BEESWING AND OLD PORT

Beeswing is a picturesque curiosity of old, bottle-aged port. It is a naturally occurring tartar deposit, distinct from the usual crust, cast by the wine as it ages, accumulating to form a delicate film that clings to the inside of the bottle. Sections of the film that detach during pouring can resemble the translucent, scale formation of a bee's wing. In the nineteenth century, it was commonly believed that the presence of beeswing denoted a port of exceptional quality.

Very old ports do not often come my way, but on one memorable occasion I thought some beeswing had. It was in Mexico. A friend clearing out the few dusty bottles in her late mother's cellar had come across a couple of ancient-looking Malagas, or maybe they were Madeira malmseys. The labels had long ago rotted away. A group of us later found a stained old cut-glass decanter in a kitchen cupboard, carefully poured the wine off its lees into it and took a glass apiece. In mine, I spied what looked like a scrap of gossamer floating on the mahogany-brown surface of the wine.

'Beeswing!' I squawked to my chums. 'It must be. I've never seen it before. How wonderful.' We all peered into the glass, and agreed. We were witnessing a rare wonder of the world of wine. I fished the delicate, translucent object out and sipped the wine. Lovely, raisiny stuff, certainly very old. Fifty years or more. We scoffed the lot. As I poured the last of it, there came an audible plop into the glass. We all peered once more, and there, floating on the wine, was the rest of the etiolated little moth that had got itself trapped in the decanter, who knows how long ago.

ROSÉ OUTLOOK

Mateus Rosé remains a respectable brand, though the wine in the distinctive bottle is now of a different style to the original sweet pink fizz launched by Portugal's Sogrape company in 1942. Fernando Guedes, son of the founder, explained the thinking behind the flask-shaped bottle: 'When my father first discussed the idea with his friends they said it would not work because it was so short you would not be able to see the bottles. But my father realised that if it was shorter, shopkeepers would have to put it in front of other bottles and it would catch the customers' eyes.'

HOLDING ON TO THE NAME

Roger Harris of Norfolk, who gave up his job with Peugeot to work in another field of French endeavour, the wines of Beaujolais, is now Britain's leading specialist merchant for the region. He told me a quaint story about one of the wines he sells. It is called Pisse Vieille, a perfectly good *cru* accounting for a fair proportion of the red wine made under the appellation of Brouilly. Long ago in the village, Roger says, an old woman went to church to make her confession. Giving her absolution, the priest enjoined the sinner, as always, '*ne piche plus*', local dialect for *ne péche plus* – sin no more. But with age she had lately grown hard of hearing. Although mystified by the misheard instruction, she took the priest at his word. She returned home and after a day or so started to behave oddly. Her husband, anguished by her growing desperation, demanded an explanation. On receiving it, he made haste to the church – and soon returned, bellowing to his wife along the length of the street as he came, '*Pisse, vieille, pisse!*' The phrase became a motto of the village.

CRACKING UP

Roger Gillett, whose Bacchus Gallery in the Sussex town of Petworth sells 'anniversary' wines, had a visit followed by a letter from the Senior Environmental Health Officer at Chichester District Council.

With assurances that the missive was not a practical joke, Mr Gillett sent me a photocopy. Part of the letter went like this: 'It was observed that you sell old and antique wines and other alcoholic drinks. E.g. Taylors Port of 1924. These old bottles are not at present labelled as to whether they are fit for human consumption or not, and it is noted that you have advised that many customers will consume such ancient brews.

'Regulation 4 of the above legislation [Food Safety (General Food Hygiene) Regulations 1995] requires that a proprietor of any food business shall assess the potential food hazards and take appropriate action to protect customers.

'Carry out an adequate assessment as to the food safety of these old bottles of alcohol. Appropriate action should be taken. Bottles should be clearly labelled "not for consumption due to age" or some such similar wording, if there is any doubt that these bottles are not safe for human consumption.'

PLAIN SPEAKING

Bill Baker was a West Country wine merchant whose appearance and manners belonged more to the eighteenth century than to our own. He died in 2008, aged only 53, and is sadly missed by most of the wine trade. In his lists of rare bottles for sale, his habit was to report plainly on bin ends he thought past their peak. As an occasional customer, I greatly enjoyed faded tawny ports and streaky white burgundies Bill had described as 'absolute rubbish' or 'crap'.

LINES IN THE VINES OF VOUVRAY

Producing wine is a major economic activity in many countries, but in France it is a way of life, and vineyards are hallowed ground. They cannot simply be ploughed up in the name of progress in the way other farmland is routinely destroyed. A *cause célèbre* in this context is the village of Vouvray, surrounded by 5,000 acres of prized vineyards, which gives its name to a venerable appellation in the Loire Valley. The Chenin Blanc grapes grown here make some of France's most distinctive wines, dry-to-sweet still whites and sparkling *vins mousseux*, from *brut* to *demi-sec*.

Vines of this variety, so local legend goes, were first planted by Roman settlers in the fourth century AD in the hospitable siliceous-clay soil that covers these gentle limestone slopes along the north bank of the river. Here too, the occupiers dug down into the hills for *tuffeau*, the alabaster-pale limestone that built the palatial villas of the declining Empire, and a thousand years later fleshed out their Renaissance successors, the fantastical riverside châteaux at Amboise and Azay-le-Rideau, Chenonceau and Cheverny, now among the most prominent national monuments of France.

The latest phase of construction in the region has been of a more prosaic kind. It began with the announcement in the mid-1980s that France's rail network, SNCF, planned to route a section of a new Paris–Bordeaux line through the very heart of the Vouvray vineyards. It would carry 30 TGV trains a day, travelling at speeds up to 186 miles per hour.

Anywhere but France, a prestige project like this would sweep all before it. But in a historic viticultural centre, resolute resistance could be anticipated. Vouvray did not disappoint. 'There have been vineyards here for more than 500 years,' local *vigneron* and firebrand Philippe Brisebarre told SNCF in his opening shot. 'You will not run TGVs through this place.'

SNCF, bolstered by the uncompromising cross-party support of the project expressed by both President François Mitterrand and his political opponent Prime Minister Jacques Chirac, demurred. M Brisebarre, who today is president of Vouvray's syndicate of wine producers, upped the ante. He led a series of noisy demonstrations by 150 growers in Vouvray: they blockaded the village square; they picketed SNCF offices; they sat down on the railway serving the nearby town of Tours, bringing chaos to the timetables. They made headlines and were invited to a live TV debate with the president of SNCF.

The demonstrators cited France's sacred, if arcane, wine laws. One of these gave the Minister of Agriculture an absolute veto on any intrusion upon vineyards classed as *appellations contrôlées*. There was a danger the Government of France could be split. SNCF was prevailed upon to make a concession.

This was duly offered. The route would be diverted underground. A new 1,500-metre tunnel, alongside the many already dug into Vouvray's hills in centuries of quarrying, would be excavated expressly for the purpose. It would cost uncountable millions. Not a fraction of vineyard would be disturbed.

If SNCF's negotiators were confident of this compromise, they were to be swiftly disillusioned. The growers protested that the *caves* (cellars) in which they matured and stored their wines in the old workings honeycombing the hills would be at risk. 'We are worried that the vibrations from the trains will accelerate the ageing of the wines,' explained Gaston Huet, Mayor of Vouvray and the region's leading winemaker. 'It's all very well for wine to age naturally, but for wine to age prematurely thanks to outside interference just won't do at all.'

The railway managers might not have believed a word of it, but they promised to commission an independent report on the likely effects of vibration on maturing wines. As a result, although the outcome of the report has never been published, a special suspension system was proposed for the underground tracks to minimize the transmission of vibration. It added more millions to the cost of the construction, but Vouvray's *vignerons* were finally mollified.

The TGV Atlantique finally went into service in 1991. Today, it carries five million passengers per year. The village of Vouvray, as I found on my last visit in 2005, has returned to its accustomed torpor. The vineyards are as plumply productive as ever, and the fruits of the harvest continue to slumber to sublime maturity, quiet in the cool darkness that prevails in the chambers of these green, unshaken hills.

NON TO UFOS IN CHÂTEAUNEUF DU PAPE

Châteauneuf du Pape in the southern Rhône valley, where the Popes of Avignon built a summer palace and surrounded it with vineyards in the fourteenth century, has always been a well-regulated sort of place. In 1923, the village's winemakers were the first in France to draw up by-laws concerning which grape varieties may be cultivated, the precise boundaries of the vineyard area, even a minimum alcohol level for the finished wine.

These regulations provided much of the basis for the national wine laws of Appellation d'Origine Contrôlée introduced throughout France in 1936. But Châteauneuf was determined to maintain the initiative. In 1954, when the post-war craze for sighting alien space-craft over Europe was at its height, the burghers of the appellation issued two solemn municipal addenda to the existing AOC. This is a simplified translation:

Article 1. Overflying, landing and taking off by airborne machines known as 'flying saucers' or 'flying cigars' of any nationality is expressly forbidden within the commune of Châteauneuf du Pape.

Article 2. Any 'flying saucer' or 'flying cigar' landing on the territory of the commune will be immediately impounded.

In commemoration of these magnificent injunctions, a Californian winemaker called Randall Grahm of the Bonny Doon vineyard at Santa Cruz produces a fine red wine in the Châteauneuf du Pape style. It is called Le Cigare Volant, the flying cigar.

ANGRY AUSTRALIANS

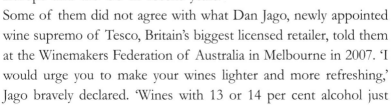

Australian winemakers are robust in defending the full-bodied and alco-holic styles that have made their fortunes in Europe and the US in recent years. Some of them did not agree with what Dan Jago, newly appointed wine supremo of Tesco, Britain's biggest licensed retailer, told them at the Winemakers Federation of Australia in Melbourne in 2007. 'I would urge you to make your wines lighter and more refreshing,' Jago bravely declared. 'Wines with 13 or 14 per cent alcohol just aren't exciting any more and customers are now looking to the Old World for more refreshing wines.' Bruce Tyrrell, a supplier of Hunter Valley wines to Tesco, reportedly had this to say: 'He's a wanker. He should go back to selling dog food. For years, Australians have been supplying the British with technically correct wines that have good colour and are full of flavour, compared with the Europeans, who have been supplying them with technically poor wines with no colour and taste like cat's piss.'

NEVER A DROP IN LANGUEDOC

Aimé Guibert makes celebrated wines at the Domaine Mas de Daumas Gassac in Languedoc. A strong believer in the integrity of French wines, he successfully frustrated a bid by California's legendary winemaker Robert Mondavi (1914–2008) to buy land near Daumas Gassac for the establishment of a new, American-style winery. Guibert is not a supporter of what he calls 'industrial' New World wines. 'Every bottle of American and Australian wine that lands in Europe,' he once said, 'is a bomb targeted at the heart of our rich European culture.'

UNBLUSHING LAURENT-PERRIER

Bernard de Nonancourt, legendary head of Laurent-Perrier, increased sales of the company's champagne from fewer than 100,000 bottles when he took over in 1949 to more than ten million bottles by the year 2000. De Nonancourt, grandson of the great Henri Lanson (who drank three bottles of his eponymous fizz every day), is fondly remembered for describing the colour

of Laurent Perrier rosé as that of *les cuisses d'une nymphe émue* – 'the thighs of an aroused nymph'. It seems unlikely we shall see his like again.

A TOUCH OF ACIDITY

I am always flattered when words I have written about wines are quoted by retailers in their lists or as 'shelf-talkers' in store. But some wine writers get shirty if their notes are lifted for these purposes, and there is now a convention that quotes from newspaper columns or books are only used with the express permission of the authors.

It is natural enough, I suppose, for writers to wish to preserve their aura of independence. Perhaps some believe that any endorsement they appear to give might have been paid for, and thus impugn their integrity.

Some writers take a more robust view than others, either way.

When he was writing about wine for the *Guardian*, Malcolm Gluck co-operated with Tesco to produce wines under the name of Superplonk, the title of his column and annual book. Several wine writers, including Jane MacQuitty of *The Times*, wondered if this might compromise his independence.

'Of course there's a conflict of interest,' Gluck retorted. 'I like conflicts of interest.'

Malcolm Gluck now writes about wine for *The Oldie*.

As the author of a current annual guide to supermarket wines, I relish memories of the clash between two predecessors in this field of endeavour. Back in the 1990s, Malcolm Gluck of *Superplonk* found himself challenged by a newcomer, Tom Stevenson, with a book cunningly entitled *SuperBooze*. In preparing his edition, Stevenson came across a problem. Sainsbury's wine boss, Allan Cheesman, was not as helpful to him as he would have liked.

'It's not just *SuperBooze* (and its readers) that Cheesman couldn't care less about,' complained Stevenson. 'I have it in writing from the man himself that he is "supporting just one guide" and that turns out to be written by Malcolm Gluck, who just happens to be the wine editor of Sainsbury's magazine, which does the integrity of both of them no good. And it does nothing for the Sainsbury family name either.'

CHABLIS, WHERE THE EARTH MOVES

The soil – *terroir* – is the big thing in French winemaking, especially in classic locations such as Chablis, at the northern extreme of Burgundy. The best vineyards here, the *grands crus*, occupy a precipitous hillside immediately north-east of the town. The soil is composed largely of fossilized Jurassic oyster shells, compacted into a barren-looking, broken shale. The roots from the Chardonnay vines wend through this ancient, jejune surface, far into the cold limestone beneath in quest of the vital nutrients that give the wine its exotic green-gold colour and unique mineral character. Each of the seven individual *grand cru* sites, although crammed together into just 247 acres all told, are said to produce wines entirely distinctive, one from the other. They are by a mile the finest and most expensive of all the wines of the Chablis appellation, which extends to 10,000 acres overall, producing wine mostly of little distinction.

The *grand cru* landscape might be prehistoric, but its permanence is not assured. Fractured by hard frosts and deluged by winter rains, the *terroir* itself is perpetually endangered. On my last visit to Chablis, on a freezing March day in 2007, Jean-Didier Basch, winemaker for Domaine Long-Depaquit, owner of the revered La Moutonne vineyard at the very heart of the hillside, explained just what the *vignerons* here have to contend with. After following him rather breathlessly up the crumbling steps that ascend La Moutonne's 30-degree gradient to the top, we turned to look out across the fabled *terroir*. We spoke of the difficulties of making wine in this harsh, exposed place, the northernmost latitude in France where grapes can be ripened sufficiently to make drinkable still wine. The vineyards are threaded with alien-looking heating devices to combat the lethal frosts, and some owners fly helicopters over the vines at dawn to stir up the freezing air in the same endeavour.

Rain, Jean-Didier added, was as much a problem as cold. In wet winters such as the one just ended, downpours could wash most of the hallowed topsoil from the slopes, dumping it in heaps at the bottom. I thought I had misheard him. But no. Was he telling me that the timeless *terroir* of Chablis' greatest vineyards had a tendency to abscond? What could they do about it? I had to know.

Did it mean that the *grands crus* might in time disappear altogether?

Monsieur Basch looked mildly surprised at my concern. 'No danger of that,' he replied. 'We just bring the lorry, shovel all the soil in, drive it round to the top of the slope, and spread it back over the vineyard.'

HARD TO SWALLOW

When I was an editor at *Reader's Digest* magazine in London, I was told that head office in the United States expected international editions to keep their readers aware of the dangers of alcohol. Articles about the hazards of 'social drinking' were regular, and hard-hitting.

I always believed this was sincere and well intentioned, but a seed of doubt has been planted by the discovery that the chairman of Reader's Digest, Thomas O. Ryder, was a considerable collector of wine. When he retired in 2007, he sold the contents of his cellar at Sotheby's in New York for $1.5 million.

MAY CONTAIN NUITS

In the years after the Second World War, wine lovers anxious to rediscover the glories of France had a particular fondness for Nuits St Georges. It might have been the evocation of England's patron saint that did the trick, but the red wines of this noble Burgundian appellation are pretty good by any standard. My maternal grand-father, Hugh Wood, who prospered by manufacturing mining machinery, liked my granny to have a glass of wine with her dinner. He always insisted on Nuits St Georges, even though he drank only

Guinness, which Granny refused to countenance. I was lucky enough to be taken by my grandparents on regular holidays, where they stayed in the best hotels, and in later years would be allowed to share Granny's wine at dinner. It was at the Savoy in London that the usual request produced a bottle of La Tâche. The sommelier wished Mr and Mrs Wood (regular guests at the hotel) to know it was one of the greatest names of Nuits St Georges. Grandpa was not impressed. He had never heard of it. Take it away, he told the sommelier, and bring us a proper Nuits St Georges. It was another 20 years before I got that close to a La Tâche again, and discovered just what Granny and I had missed.

SPREADING THE WORD

I have always treasured an item of wine advice published in *Airmail*, the newspaper of Newcastle Airport. 'Once you've discovered the wonder of wine, one of the best things to do is to get to know your grape varieties,' the writer counselled. He particularly commended what he called the undervalued noble grape of Germany: 'Go for a Riesling from the Moslem region and you'll soon be converted.'

LOSING IT

As a consumer writer, I have received and sympathized with many anguished complaints from readers about the service received from wine merchants. After relating these outrages in newspaper and magazine columns, I have occasionally received lively rebuttals from the merchants. Here, the complainant asserted, was a compounded but representative dialogue with a mail-order customer:

Ah, yes, about your order . . . you know, the one you forgot to place, but are nonetheless going to be awfully braying and petulant about when you ring and tell me it hasn't yet been delivered, even though you are convinced you placed the order weeks ago, despite the fact that I have your signed order form here, in front of me, which is dated Tuesday of this week, but your memory is absolutely perfect about when you sent the order, because you remember that you saw the advertisement in that awfully nice magazine about pig breeding which you were reading in the vet's when Henry, your Labrador, had to go in and be done, and so it must be at least four weeks ago and it really isn't good enough and you are not really interested in excuses or the fact that we didn't advertise in *Pig Breeders Weekly*, and, by the way, who was that case of wine from which was delivered yesterday, because you would like to thank them for it, but there wasn't a card or note attached, but you don't recall ordering it on the 5th, and I am terribly sorry madam that your order has already been delivered, but sadly we process the orders as they come in and we hadn't realized that you specifically wanted it delivered on Christmas morning, and have you possibly counted the number of bottles you have received and I am sure you have what you ordered and I am genuinely sorry, but yours is the only order which we haven't managed to get delivered in time for Christmas which I do realize is disappointing, but the carriers have let us down on this one.

JUST IN CASE . . .

The Wine Society has reported some of the instructions members give on their order forms for delivery drivers in the event of there being nobody home. Included are:

Please . . .
 . . . leave by front door in plain wrap marked 'caution, swine fever'.
 . . . leave at back door but not in front of cat flap.
 . . . leave in dustbin, not Tuesdays.
 . . . leave in Wendy house.
 . . . leave in dog kennel.
 . . . leave in the pub.
 . . . leave in fish and chip shop.
 . . . leave at number 12. Knock hard.
 . . . leave in outbuildings; if geese approach just shoo them away.

. . . leave with any neighbour.
. . . do not leave with neighbours.

ROEDERER RAP

Champagne Louis Roederer found its way into the headlines in 2006 thanks to an interview given by its boss, Frédéric Rouzaud, to the *Economist* magazine. Asked what he made of the mascot status his premium brand Cristal enjoyed in American rap and hip-hop culture, Rouzaud said he viewed the phenomenon with 'curiosity and serenity'. Did he worry that the association might harm Cristal's good name? 'That's a good question,' he responded. 'But what can we do. We can't forbid people from buying it.'

Rouzaud may have had in mind the fact that some performers were writing the name of his product into their lyrics, as in rapper Jay-Z's immortal line 'Let's sip the Cris and get pissy pissy' in his chart-topping song 'Hard Knock Life'. What he seems less likely to have had in mind was that after his interview with the *Economist* reached a wider audience, the same Jay-Z would pronounce him a racist and boycott Louis Roederer champagne.

But that is exactly what Jay-Z, who is a club owner as well as an entertainer and all-round entrepreneur, did. He transferred his allegiances to rival champagne brands, and has since lent his name in a much more formal sense to other drinks, including Budweiser beer. I met Rouzaud briefly in 2007 at a London tasting of Cristal wines, and while he looked momentarily sad at the mention of all the fuss, he seemed sanguine. The Louis Roederer company has had its ups and downs before.

Rouzaud told the story: Roederer was founded in 1776, and is still family owned. He is the great-grandson of Camille Olry-Roederer, who in 1932 became the second wife of company owner Léon Olry-Roederer and, three months later, his widow. 'She didn't kill him,' Rouzaud hastily added, 'and the company was not at that time a good thing to inherit, because of the economic depression and the loss of the Russian business.'

Russia had long been Roederer's main export market. The Cristal brand was created and bottled in crystal-clear glass at the request of champagne-aficionado Tsar Alexander in 1876. It was supplied exclusively to his court until it all ended abruptly with the Russian Revolution of 1917. 'We were selling more than 600,000 bottles, a quarter of all the champagne we made, to Russia,' said Mr Rouzaud, 'and then zero for the rest of the century.'

Even now, sales to Russia have returned to only a modest 40,000 bottles a year. But elsewhere, in a process begun by Rouzaud's enterprising great-granny Camille, who ran Roederer single-handed until 1975, the name has gone round the world, and created the Cristal cult of today.

The Roederer history is as much one of survival as it is of triumph, and while most businesses now seem to thrive only on perpetual expansion, this company is today making no more champagne than it did in the nineteenth century, about 2.5 million bottles a year. Most of this is accounted for by the non-vintage Brut Premier wine, with Cristal production varying wildly from year to year according to the prevailing conditions of each vintage in the highly rated *grand cru* vineyards, all owned by Roederer, from which the grapes come. In 2002, they made 800,000 bottles of Cristal, but in 1998 none. Some years produce no more than 100,000 bottles.

Is the price of Cristal worth paying? If you're a millionaire, you won't care, but if you simply enjoy champagne and are curious to know what the 'top of the top, the cream of the cream' (as Rouzaud describes Cristal) actually tastes like, could you justify laying out a week's housekeeping money for the privilege?

My answer is yes. I was won over by the enthusiasm, and the good humour, with which Messrs Rouzaud and his winemaker Jean-Baptiste Lecaillon described the painstaking business of making this wine. I was persuaded that at Roederer, they don't cut corners. Unlike most well-known wine producers, they are not part of a multinational corporation and in thrall to the balance sheet. Frédéric Rouzaud puts it well: 'We have the freedom in a family company to be concerned only with the quality of the wine.'

We tasted Cristal from the 1999 and 2000 vintages and five other years back to 1979. Jean-Baptiste Lecaillon described the 1999 wine as 'very soft, very gentle, very round, very seductive' and I will not gainsay him. The other vintages were equally convincing in their different ways, with the overall theme that the older the wines are, the more extraordinary they taste.

I was completely taken in. Louis Roederer Cristal might be outrageously expensive, but it's outrageously good, too. Even in hard times, if we have something special to celebrate we should not hesitate to blow the housekeeping on a bottle of a wine. We all need mad moments in our lives from time to time, and this one fits the bill.

THE FAT BASTARD

Silly names for wines are a relatively new phenomenon, ushered in with the present and worryingly persistent era of brands. From earlier, more innocent times I fondly remember Australia's Kanga Rouge, Algeria's Red Infuriator and, still going strong, Goats du Roam, a South African spin on Côtes du Rhône by a winemaker called Charles Back who really does run a herd of goats at his vineyard. I am less keen on contrived names like Cat's Pee on a Gooseberry

Bush, an alleged metaphor for the smell of the wine, a Sauvignon Blanc from New Zealand. And I hate Fat Bastard, a coarse name for a Chardonnay from the Languedoc region of France. When this wine first made it on to supermarket shelves (to my surprise in a censorious age) I asked the British importer, Guy Anderson, who worked with winemaker Thierry Boudinaud to produce it, how the name had been arrived at.

Anderson recalled a day in the cellars: 'I handed Thierry a glass of my favourite blend and asked him what he thought of it. Now Thierry has made wine all over the world and in his travels has picked up a fair dose of Aussie winery lingo. So if you can imagine for a moment a Frenchman with a thick Aussie accent, he turned to me and said, "Well, mate, I'll tell you this . . . it's a real fat bastard of a Chardonnay . . . I love it!"

'For six months we tried to think up a proper name for the wine then we thought, Sod it, if they can have Bâtard Montrachet in Burgundy then why can't the Languedoc have a Fat Bastard Chardonnay? It's as simple as that.'

GNATS PISS AND OTHER NAMES

There was, briefly, a Sauvignon–Sémillon blend from the Entre Deux Mers region south of Bordeaux called Gnats Piss, made by the entirely respectable Jean Louis Despagne, but it did not last. In 2008, Languedoc producer Jean-Marc Speziale released some of his wine under the label Vin de Merde and reportedly sold 5,000 bottles, but whether this stunt can perpetuate itself remains to be seen. Maybe it will, as post-modern ironic brands such as Old Git and Old Tart (both French) and Pansy Rosé (New Zealand) have lingered for years.

TOUGH AS OLD PORTS

Does port go off once it's been opened? If left to languish in a decanter for weeks on end it probably will, but some old ports can be impressively robust. Anthony Barnes, a Master of Wine who works for the auctioneers Bonhams, regularly catalogues the cellars of house-holders who wish to sell their wines. In one, a bin containing vintage ports from the 1920s included a couple of bottles with broken wax seals. 'They had been opened probably fifty years before our visit. A glass or two had been drunk from each and the corks simply pushed back in,' Anthony told me. 'I asked the owner if we might taste these wines. Both bottles, I'm happy to say, were in perfect condition, as if they had never been disturbed.'

SUNK

Jacques Cousteau (1910–97), hero of the French Resistance, pioneer of scuba-diving and the most famous of all undersea explorers, once found a bottle of Roman wine on the Mediterranean seabed.

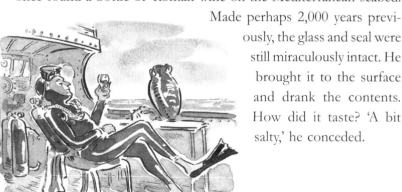

Made perhaps 2,000 years previously, the glass and seal were still miraculously intact. He brought it to the surface and drank the contents. How did it taste? 'A bit salty,' he conceded.

A WEE BIT OF PORTIFICATION

All wines are blends. Because it says French, Chilean or Malagassy on the label doesn't even guarantee it is all from the nation in question, let alone from the nominated region, grape variety or vintage. Winemakers with a formula and a budget in mind will blend in whatever is necessary to come up with a finished product that looks, smells and tastes as good as it can for the price.

This is all obvious enough. But the art of blending need not be confined to the winery. You can do it at home. I had a very constructive letter from a reader, Ian Colquhoun of Glasgow, who told me about his own method.

'What a disappointment it is when a bottle of red wine turns out to be weedy and thin, but my experience, perhaps due to the economies I must take when calling at the offie, is that too many do. This is why I keep a bottle of cooking port handy for the rescuing of emaciated wines,' Mr Colquhoun reported. 'I estimate that a £5 bottle of supermarket ruby will stretch to about eight bottles. I add an inch or so to the bottle then give it a good shake.

'I like to think of it,' he added with sudden inspiration, 'as the antithesis of Charles Lamb's motto that a mixture of brandy and water spoils two good things. Powering up your plonk with a lash of dodgy port makes a positive virtue of two bad things.'

PUTTING A CORK IN IT

'Vintage' wine aged in glass rather than wood is a relatively recent notion, enabled by the introduction of a new type of bottle in the late eighteenth century. Cylindrical with a straight, narrow neck that could be stoppered with a long, driven cork, the bottles could be stacked on their sides, keeping the wine in contact with the cork to prevent it drying out and shrinking.

The first 'vintage' wine shipped under an identifiable name in bottles rather than casks is claimed by the company of George Sandeman & Co to have been its 1790 Port, bottled in 1792. The first vintage of claret to get the treatment is generally agreed to have been the 1798. Château Margaux of this year was selling in London in 1802 (the year of its bottling) at £9 2s 6d a dozen. Based on average earnings then and now, that price would currently equate to £4,000 – just about the going rate for new vintages of Margaux today.

NAME-DROPPING

Champagne is a national treasure of France, so why do so many of its famous brands sound German? Bollinger, Heidsieck, Krug, Mumm, Roederer and others hardly resound to the beat of the Gallic drum. The answer is that when the sparkling wine became popular in the eighteenth century, few local *vignerons* had the skills needed to make it. So the families who owned the land and merchant businesses recruited winemakers from Germany to do the job. When it came to naming the individual *maisons* and their products, the aristocratic landowners and bourgeois merchants considered it *de trop* to append their own names and co-opted those of their winemakers instead.

NAZI ONSLAUGHT

Grapes are relished by all sorts of creatures. Starlings are notorious in England for stripping vines and France's *vignerons* are frequently called to arms to repel sweet-toothed wild boars. In South Africa,

baboons present the same problem, and can prove a lot more difficult to deter. But perhaps the oddest of the predators are the Nazi
raccoons of Germany. Hermann Goering, so the story goes,
imported the animals in 1934 in a bid to boost species diversity in
the national fauna. The North-American incomers, being om-
nivorous and nocturnal, have proved remarkably persistent. There
are now said to be a million of them loose in Germany. In a 2005
raid shortly before harvest time in Brandenburg, a horde of several
thousand raccoons consumed an entire vineyard's fruit in a matter
of days.

BLEATING ABOUT THE LABEL

At Château Mouton Rothschild, where a new label design has been
commissioned each year since 1945 to a different artist, there came
an awkward interruption with the 1993 vintage. The design for the
year was a pencil portrait by octogenarian artist Balthazar Klossowski
de Rola, better known as Balthus, of a nude, adolescent girl. In the
United States, outraged lobbyists persuaded the Bureau of Alcohol,
Tobacco and Firearms that the label was an incitement to child
abuse, and the 30,000 bottles destined for the American market
had to be stripped of their
labels. Reprints, minus the
image, were substi-
tuted. Balthus declined
to make any comment.

The French relish their class distinctions with true republican zeal. The *Cru Classé* systems of ranking wine estates in Bordeaux and other regions are no exception. The first of them was devised for the 1855 Great Exhibition staged in Paris at the behest of Napoleon III, nephew of Bonaparte, who had been President of the Second Republic but in 1852 got himself elected Emperor. He wished to show off the bounty of France to the wider world, and particularly to Britain, which had afforded him political asylum and generous hospitality during his years of exile.

Bordeaux wines were a major interest of the Emperor's, and a correspondingly prominent feature of the exhibition. As a promotional wheeze, the top 62 estates of the principal red-wine region, the Médoc, were listed by the Bordeaux Chamber of Commerce in five divisions for the show. The term *cru classé* or 'classed growth' – *cru* being an all-encompassing term for a vineyard and its product – had been in use a long time, and the grading of the Médoc's top estates into five classes dated back to the previous century, but had not been formalized before. Ranks were based on the most recent prices fetched on the Bordeaux market for the wines of the respective châteaux, starting with the four *premiers grands crus classés* of Lafite, Latour, Margaux and Haut-Brion and working on down through the 15 *deuxièmes*, 14 *troisièmes*, 11 *quatrièmes* and 18 *cinquièmes*.

The great châteaux of the Sauternes, producers of sweet white wines, were also classified for the 1855 exhibition, but the other major Bordeaux regions of Graves and St Emilion had to wait a century for their turns, in 1953 and 1955 respectively. In the meantime, a number of owners in the Médoc who had been left out of the original classification and who called themselves *crus bourgeois* (without a trace of irony – this is France), had formed themselves into a syndicate and were working on making this rank official. In 1932, no fewer than 443 names were listed as *crus bourgeois supérieurs exceptionnels* (only six merited this lofty status), *crus bourgeois supérieurs* (100 qualifiers) or *crus bourgeois* (337). In subsequent reclassifications, the total number of *crus bourgeois* fell sharply – to 290 in 1943 (about 150 estates had gone bust) and 127 in 1977. The listings have been reviewed occasionally by the syndicate according to how good the wines are deemed in tastings organized for the purpose. But

this system fell apart in 2003 when several châteaux were demoted in, or entirely from, a list now grown to 247, thanks to the boom years in Bordeaux that started in the 1980s. But some owners challenged the legitimacy of the tastings, taking their grievances to law. France's agriculture ministry now became involved and in 2007 the classification was annulled altogether. A new form of classification was under consideration by 2009, but it could be some time before the term *crus bourgeois* reappears on labels.

This sad turn of events brings to an unhappy conclusion a deliciously quirky and utterly French piece of class discrimination. It is a comfort, though, that the original 1855 classification of the grandest names of the Médoc and Sauternes is still in full sail. Every single one of the estates listed is still in business, and prospering as never before.

Many of the châteaux of Bordeaux, whether *premiers crus*, humble (former) *crus bourgeois* or estates of no classification whatever, have their own idiosyncratic little stories to tell. Following is a random collection of châteaux curiosities collected along the way:

Château d'Armailhac, a *5ième cru* in Pauillac, owes its origins to a sleazy aristocrat, Dominique d'Armailhacq (pronounced AR-my-yak). In the 1730s he bought a vineyard close to the great estate of Mouton, and set about enlarging it to an economic size. This he did by lending money to the peasants living on the surrounding land and evicting them when they couldn't meet the usurious repayments. He grandly named the estate Mouton-d'Armailhacq, but the 'château' today testifies to his heirs' financial failure; it has remained only half-built since the family ran out of cash in the 1820s and is one of the real architectural curios of the region. The property was bought in 1933 by Mouton owner Baron Philippe Rothschild, who, with customary self-effacement, changed its name to Château Mouton Baron Philippe in 1956, then to Mouton Baronne Philippe in 1976 to commemorate his wife, Baronne Pauline, who died in that year. Baronne Philippine Rothschild, who inherited the estate on her father's death in 1988, restored the name d'Armailhac (dropping the 'q') to the estate with the 1989 vintage. The wine is made at Mouton.

Château Ausone, along with Cheval Blanc, is one of the only two *premiers grands crus* of St Emilion with the supreme rating 'A' appended to their classification. A tiny vineyard producing only 20,000 or so bottles of very expensive wine each year, its name commemorates Decimus Magnus Ausonius. A Roman citizen born in Bordeaux about AD 310, he founded the school of rhetoric in the city in 334, and wrote widely on natural sciences, including viticulture. He also produced a lot of bad poetry, some of it pornographic. In later life he was summoned to Rome to become tutor to emperor-in-waiting Gratian, and on the prince's accession was rewarded with high offices including Consul, and Governor of Gaul. When Gratian was murdered after a four-year reign in 383, Ausonius retired to his Bordeaux estate, supposedly the site of the present château, until his death aged 85 in 395.

Château Batailley, a *5ième cru* in Pauillac, is said to be on the site of a murderous rout suffered by English troops at the climax of the Hundred Years War in 1453. The house stands amidst a magnificent park laid out, with melancholy appropriateness, in the English fashion. A more prosaic explanation for the name is that the estate was once owned by Joseph Batailhé, wine merchant to King Charles II of England.

Château Belgrave, a *5ième cru* in St Laurent, has a label that sports a snooty-looking dachshund, making this wine the ideal choice for lovers of these charming little dogs. Once described by America's leading wine critic Robert Parker as 'consistently mediocre', Belgrave

was bought in 1998 by Bordeaux négociant Dourtne, and it now makes better wines than in the past.

Château Beychevelle, a *4ième cru*, takes its name from a Gascon dialect version of the French *baisse voiles* or 'lower sails'. The story goes that the estate, standing in St Julien with commanding views over the river Gironde, was once the property of an admiral of the French fleet, the Duc d'Epernon. Naval vessels passing by were expected to salute the great man by dipping their sails. Beychevelle's label accordingly depicts an ancient galley with furled sail. Beychevelle's present owner is the Japanese brewer-distiller Suntory.

Château Branaire-Ducru, a *4ième cru* in St Julien, has a reputation for tasting of chocolate. And it has another claim to fame. The late wine-loving author Roald Dahl gave Branaire the pivotal role in his classic short story of greed and lust, *The Wine Taster*. Against his host at a dinner party, a loathsome gourmet bets his worldly goods that he can identify the claret being served. The host's nubile daughter is horrified when her father agrees to pledge her virtue as his side of the wager. The villain, who has of course slyly inspected the bottle's label beforehand, successfully nominates Branaire-Ducru 1934. Happily, his intended victim is rescued at the last minute by the discovery of the subterfuge.

Château Brane-Cantenac, a *2ième cru* in Margaux, is by far the most productive of the *grands crus classés*, turning out as many as half a million bottles from a single harvest. The name dates from 1833 when the estate, then called Gorce-Guy, was bought by Baron Joseph Hector de Brane. The Baron, who had introduced the Cabernet Sauvignon grape to the Médoc and was locally known as 'the Napoleon of the Vines', had lately sold the famed Mouton estate (then Brane-Mouton, of course) which his family had elevated to great status in the previous century. Joseph Hector set out to repeat the formula with the Cantenac property, but with comparatively modest success. He sold out, for a million francs, to a syndicate in 1866.

Château Calon-Ségur, a *3ième cru* in St Estèphe, has a distinctive label bearing the outline of a heart. This commemorates the Marquis Nicholas-Alexandre de Ségur, who owned not just this relatively humble property, but Châteaux Lafite, Latour and Mouton, too. The Marquis, who died in 1755, once remarked: 'I make my wine at Lafite and Latour, but my heart is at Calon.' The name Calon is said to derive from a local term meaning a wood, but it is a curious co-incidence that *calon* is the Welsh word for heart. In an interview with newspaper *Le Figaro*, actor Johnny Depp revealed that Calon-Ségur is his favourite wine, ahead even of Cheval Blanc and Pétrus.

Château Camensac, a *5ième cru* in St Laurent, was the first of the Médoc *crus classés* to employ mechanical harvesters in its vineyards. The practice, which has not caught on among the neighbours, was initiated by Enrique Forner, who bought Camensac in 1964. He went on to found a rather larger enterprise, Marques de Caceres in Spain's Rioja region.

Château Cantemerle, a *5ième cru* in the commune of Macau, is a delightfully romantic turreted mansion set in dense woodland.

This nineteenth-century fantasy replaced an ancient fortress where in the early 1400s a mob of occupying English troops encamped, broke into the cellars, and turned nasty. In the castle grounds stood a huge, sooty cannon affectionately known as the *merle* – blackbird – and this the estate workers primed, loaded and fired in the direction of the enemy. The cannon exploded into pieces with such violence that the English feared a full-scale artillery bombardment, and fled. The property was saved, and in commemoration of this unexpected outcome was renamed *cante merle* – the blackbird's song.

Château Chasse-Spleen is not a *cru classé* but once enjoyed the grandiloquent and now redundant classification of *cru grand bourgeois exceptionnel.* The estate, in the commune of Moulis, is said to have acquired its name from a brush with the nobility. In 1821, when it was known as Grand-Poujeaux, the château had a visit from Lord Byron. The poet, then the greatest celebrity of the day, liked the wine so much that he declared 'it chases away my spleen'.

Château Cheval Blanc is a *premier grand cru classé* and the leading estate of St Emilion, so-called because it is on the site once occupied by a staging post en route between Navarre (on the Spanish side of the Pyrenees) and Paris where King Henry IV of France, who always rode white horses, would change mounts. The Cheval Blanc 1947 is regularly trotted out as the greatest claret ever made. Jancis Robinson is among the wine gurus who support the assertion, and the hit movie *Sideways* wrote the notion into its script. About 20 years ago, I had a glass or two of the '47 with shepherd's pie in front of the telly at the home of a hospitable City friend in Putney. We agreed that it was peculiarly dense, reminiscent of port rather than claret, and weirdly vigorous for its age.

Château Ducru-Beaucaillou, a *2ième cru* in St Julien, gets its forename from Bertrand Ducru, who bought the vineyard in 1795. The estate was already known as Beaucaillou, meaning 'beautiful pebble' in an apt description of the unusually large stones that naturally form the surface matter of this riverside property. M. Ducru's predecessor had changed the name from Maucaillou, 'bad pebble', given to the vineyard long before, when it was assumed that such stony ground could not be ideal for wine-grape growing. In fact, as the enlightened winemakers of the late eighteenth century were discovering, the more barren the *terroir* looks, the more beautiful the wine might just turn out to be.

Château Haut Brion is the only one of 62 Bordeaux estates included in the original 1855 classification that is not in the Médoc, the great vineyard region to the north of the city of Bordeaux. Haut Brion lies in the commune of Pessac-Léognan within the area known as the Graves, south of the city. It was included, as one of only four *premiers crus*, simply on merit. Its wines were then fetching prices just as high as those for Lafite, Latour and Margaux. No other wine outside the Médoc at that time came close even to the fifth growths for price. Haut Brion has the distinction of being the first individual estate wine mentioned in English literature. Samuel Pepys named it in his diary entry for 10 April 1663 as 'a sort of French wine, called Ho Bryan, that hath a good and most particular taste that I never met with.' Back then, Haut Brion was owned by the Pontac family, whose estates in Bordeaux were so numerous that the name Pontac was often used in place of the generic 'claret'. The château last changed hands in the 1930s, when it was bought for the equivalent of £100,000 by American banker Clarence Dillon. Many Bordeaux properties were up for sale at that time of economic slump, and it is said Dillon was really looking to buy Cheval Blanc in St Emilion. But his chauffeur got lost in the fog on the day they set out from the city of Bordeaux, and Dillon settled for Haut Brion because it was the nearest *premier cru* to the city centre. Dillon died in 1979, aged 96, and the estate is still owned by his heirs.

Château Lagrange, a *3ième cru* in St Julien, is owned by the Japanese distiller and brewer Suntory. Another peculiarity is the château itself. About 1750, the old castle was torn down and replaced with a sublimely symmetrical, classical pedimented house. After the French Revolution, the estate came into the hands of Jean-Valère Caburrus.

Enriched through the patronage of Napoleon Bonaparte, who put him in charge of the finances of occupied Spain, Caburrus built a bizarre extension on to the house – a huge, four-storey Italianate tower. I used to believe it was self-consciousness about this monstrosity that drove subsequent owners of Lagrange to keep the image of the house very small on the label, dwarfed by two Disney-esque medieval knights-in-armour placed either side. But since the 1990s, the management has dumped the knights and put a new, architectural print of the ludicrous building absolutely centre stage. Have they no shame?

Château Lynch-Bages, a *5ième cru* in Pauillac, is fondly known to the fast-shrinking public-school element in the British wine trade as 'lunch bags'. The name Lynch has a story behind it. John Lynch was an Irish patriot who fought, aged 21, for the exiled James II against the forces of King Billy (the Dutchman William III of England) at the Battle of the Boyne in 1690. After the rout, Lynch escaped aboard a French troopship evacuating the Catholic battalions sent by Louis XIV in support of the Jacobites. He settled in Bordeaux, married a local girl and had two sons, one of whom, Thomas, in turn married. His bride unexpectedly inherited the great wine estate of Domaine de Batges, as it was then known, of which Thomas became master, in 1749, appending the family name.

Château Margaux, one of the four original *premiers grands crus* of the 1855 classfication, has been a farm since the twelfth century and has made wine since the 1560s. It has had some colourful owners. The present splendid château, familiar from the label with its grand pediment supported by four Doric columns, was completed in 1810 for the Marquis de Colonilla, who had acquired it cheap after its seizure in the Revolution. He had the fabled earlier house demolished without ever having seen it. Previous owner Elie Du Barry, brother-in-law of the King's mistress, had acquired Margaux through marriage, but fled the country, leaving his wife to the mercy of the Guillotine. The last change of ownership was in 1977, when the estate was put up for sale, attracting bids from buyers worldwide. The highest came from America, but the French government intervened, insisting

that Margaux was a national treasure and should not fall into foreign hands. The final purchaser was the owner of a chain of French supermarkets, a Mr Mentzelopoulos. No one seemed to notice that he was Greek.

Château Montrose is a *2ième cru* but a relative newcomer. The estate was first planted about 1815, on a hill previously covered with heather – thus the name, from the pink flowers – and the estate, in St Estèphe, has been known as Montrose only since 1825. Perhaps it was the British-sounding name (Montrose is an excellent wee royal borough in Tayside) that encouraged the Germans to commandeer the estate during the Second World War. The working buildings became a Wehrmacht artillery post, and part of the grounds was used as a rifle range. In 1942 an RAF bomber cratered the vineyard, apparently mistaking it for the Shell oil refinery at Pauillac, more than two miles away.

Château Palmer Charles Palmer came from a wealthy brewing family in the city of Bath in the west of England. His father wanted him to go into the Church, but obligingly died and left him not just the brewery but Bath's Theatre Royal, and £100,000. Charles became MP for Bath by giving free admission to the theatre to the city's 30 electors (all doctors) and bought a commission in the 10th Hussars. He rose to the rank of major-general during the Peninsular War and was among the force that marched into Bordeaux in 1814. Commanded urgently to Paris, General Palmer took a coach for the three-day journey. On board was an attractive young widow, Marie Brunet de Ferrière, who regaled him with a woeful tale. Her late husband had died a broken man, ruined by the exigencies of the war. She was hurrying to the capital to sell her only legacy, the great wine estate of Château de Gascq in Cantenac-Margaux, which she assured him was second in reputation only to Château Lafite. Palmer was beguiled. History does not record all that took place on the journey, but by the end of it, he was the new owner of the Château.

Giving his own name to the property and its wine, the General invested heavily, extending the vineyards and stepping up production. Quality was said to be excellent. Château Palmer soon arrived in London, where it became fashionable in the clubs and officers' messes. The Prince Regent, an acquaintance and fellow Hussar, threw a dinner at Carlton House to introduce the wine into his circle. But the Prince pronounced the wine too slight for his taste and suggested to Palmer he should to try making something a bit heftier, like his own preferred 'claret', a souped-up concoction called Carbonel sourced largely in the Rhône.

Idiotically, the General took this advice to heart. He tore up his vines, spent a fortune (much of it embezzled by his estate manager) on replanting and re-equipping, and in the process ruined both himself and the reputation of the estate. Château Palmer was sold to his creditors in 1843, and the General died, bankrupt, two years later.

Palmer had only partially recovered its good name by 1855, the year of the classification, and thus was ranked a third growth, instead of the *deuxième* or even the *premier cru* status to which it might have once aspired.

Château Pichon-Longueville Comtesse de Lalande in Pauillac, a leading *2ième cru*, owes its present eminence to May-Eliane de Lencquesaing, who became the sole owner in 1978. Pichon-Lalande fell to her by chance in a divvy-up with her brother and sister. They had inherited several properties from their parents and decided to allocate them by lot. At the time, Mme de Lencquesaing was disappointed with her ticket, drawn from a biscuit tin; she would have preferred the Paris apartment. But she transformed the estate, and on retirement sold it to the Louis Roederer champagne company in 2007 for 180 million euros.

Château Le Pin in Pomerol is, in some vintages, the most expensive of all Bordeaux wines. The original vineyard, a single hectare of Merlot neighbouring Vieux Chateau Certan, was bought by Jacques Thienpoint, whose father ran VCC, in 1979 for a million francs; it has been enlarged to nearly two hectares since, with the acquisition of an adjacent vegetable garden and an acre bought from the Pomerol blacksmith. The vintage that made Le Pin famous, the 1982, went on to the market at just £100 a case, rising to £300 (at Christie's) in 1985 and £18,000 by 1997. Current price is estimated at £40,000. Jacques Thienpoint sold out the 1982 long ago and now has only

one bottle, bought for him by his Scottish wife Fiona at an auction in 2006.

Château Pontet Canet, a *5ième cru* in Pauillac, is a pioneer in environmentally friendly grape-growing. Owner Guy Tesseron has dispensed with diesel-guzzling tractors for hoeing between the vines and has brought in three shire horses. They are called Babette, Kakou and Reine.

Château Smith Haut-Lafitte in the Graves has been producing wine since 1365. The Anglo element of the name recalls George Smith, a Scots shipowner who bought the vineyard in the 1700s, built the present hunting-lodge-like house and dispatched all the wine home to Scotland in his own ship. The owners since 1990 have been Daniel Cathiard, a former Olympic skier for France, and his wife Florence. Very unusually for a great wine estate in Bordeaux, they have established a luxury hotel, Les Sources de Caudalie, adjacent to the château, complete with a Michelin-starred restaurant. Even more extraordinary, the Cathiards' daughter Mathilde operates a health spa at the château, which offers *vinothérapie* to 'relax, slow down the ageing process and lose weight'. It has been so successful that Mathilde has started several other spas around the world. In the best tradition, the hotel also has a *Tour des Cigares* in which smokers can enjoy a Havana 'with a panoramic view over the vineyards'.

Château Talbot Sisters Lorraine and Nancy Cordier have run this St Julien *4ième cru* estate, along with several others, since their father Jean died in 1993. It is named in honour of John Talbot, the Earl of Shrewsbury, who commanded the last English army in Bordeaux at the end of the Hundred Years War in 1453. He was defeated and killed at the battle of Castillon on 17 July in that year, bringing to an end his country's dominion over Bordeaux. The winemakers of the region, dependent on trade with England, were very sorry to see him go.

DANISH PROTOCOL

My wife Sheila was born in Copenhagen, and we once had a wonderful holiday there. A high point was our day out on the train to Helsingor, the Elsinore of Shakespeare's *Hamlet*, where the monumental castle of Kronborg still glowers across the strait at Sweden.

Here, from a well-informed and good-humoured guide in the banqueting hall, we enjoyed hearing about the good old days of courtly hospitality in Denmark. King Frederik II, who built the castle, celebrated his coronation there in 1559 with a feast at which the guests drank 32,000 litres of Rhenish (German) wine and incalculable quantities of the local schnapps spirit. After each toast, it was the custom to throw the glasses either into the fireplaces or out of the windows. At the coronation of King Kristian IV in 1596, according to the guide, 35,000 glasses were disposed of in this way and every single pane of window glass in the castle was broken.

Castle banquets must have been memorable. Typically, the guests spent five to six hours at table, ate eight kilograms of food and drank between five and seven litres of beer. But best manners were still demanded. The castle rules enjoined: 'One must not be choosy and one must not put what one could not eat on one's neighbour's plate. In addition there is to be no fighting or knocking over of the drinking jug.'

'Getting drunk at banquets was nothing to be ashamed of,' our guide told us. 'One guest described how he found the whole company on the floor "buried in sleep and wine". The drunkenness was not restricted to men. Women and children too could join in.'

Kristian IV, who was on the Danish throne at the time Shakespeare was writing *Hamlet*, introduced the rowdy custom of accompanying the drinking of loyal toasts with drum rolls and trumpet blasts (and even the occasional round of cannon fire), just as portrayed in the play.

STARTS AND STOPS

The word 'corkscrew', according to the Oxford dictionaries, dates only from 1720. That's more than a century after the introduction of cork bungs for wine bottles. The first corks were probably employed in England in the early 1600s, fashioned from cork-oak-bark imported from Portugal and Spain (just as now) for closing bottles of sack, the muddy precursor of sherry. The corks were driven only part way into the bottle's neck to avoid putting too much stress on the delicate glass of the time and, no doubt, to facilitate withdrawal.

The invention of the corkscrew is shrouded in the mists of time. It was not an original idea, but based on the very long helix or 'worm' used for extracting wadding and shot from the barrels of muskets when they failed to discharge. In seventeenth-century writings, the cork-pulling adaptation is described as a 'bottlescrew'. Curiously, this word now no longer appears in newer editions of the Oxford dictionaries at all.

BANG GOES THE CORK

The pressure inside a champagne bottle, so they say, is at the same level to which the tyre of a double-decker bus is inflated. Ease off the wire cage,* give the bottle a good shake and the cork can be expected to travel a bit. The first person to propel a champagne cork a confirmed distance of over 100 feet was Gary Mahan of California on 2 August 1975. His cork went 102 feet 11 inches, and won a place in the *Guinness Book of Records*. The record was extended to 177 feet 9 inches by Professor Heinrich Medicus on 5 June 1988 in New York State and remains officially unbroken because the *Guinness Book of Records* no longer reports this achievement. Too silly, no doubt.

STAR RATINGS

There is a curious synergy between celebrity and wine. Actors, musicians and sports stars in particular seem to relish the association,

---

*The wire cage or *muselet* was invented in 1844 by Adolfe Jacquesson, whose eponymous champagne house is still very much in business today.

either by endorsing existing brands or buying their own vineyards. The late Paul Newman had his own vineyard in California and Dan Aykroyd's name appears above the titles of several American wines including Signature Reserve VQA Niagara Peninsula Vidal Ice Wine, which seems enough of a mouthful as it is. Rather more hip is a range of wines under the K'Orus label lately launched by former Motown Records boss Kedar Massenberg, who says they are 'targeted to the trendsetting African-American consumer and other novice wine drinkers'.

In Australia, the 'Great White Shark' of golf, Greg Norman, has a major wine business, also with connections in California, and in New Zealand, Ulster-born actor Sam Neill makes good Pinot Noir reds at his Two Paddocks vineyard in Central Otago. Next door, his chum Roger Donaldson, who directed *Sleeping Dogs*, the film that made Neill famous, is also busy making wine. The name on the label of his Chardonnay is, suitably enough, Sleeping Dogs.

Over in Europe, American actors Johnny Depp and Brad Pitt and their respective partners Vanessa Paradis and Angelina Jolie have both bought estates with vineyards in southern France, but it is far too early to be looking forward to wines made under their names. Mick Hucknall, retiring vocalist with pop group Simply Red, is rather further ahead with his vineyard in Sicily. The estate, on the slopes of Mount Etna, makes well-reviewed wines under the estate's name, Il Cantante – the singer.

French screen giant Gérard Depardieu has been making his own wines for nearly 30 years and now has vineyards in Bordeaux and the Languedoc as well as outposts in Argentina, Spain and Morocco. Depardieu, as I discovered in a brief encounter at a tasting of his wines in London in 2005, is a disarming man. His fame and sheer physical presence might tend to overawe, but he is also possessed of a cheerful candour I have not invariably encountered in French winemakers. He is used to being asked daft questions about what it's like to be in the limelight one minute and alone among the vines the next. He made even the most po-faced of my wine-writing colleagues smile when he described his philosophy to us: 'Believe it or not, I can be happy on this earth with very little, but I like to have a lot in my glass.'

FROTHING AT THE MOUTH

Prosecco, the softly sparkling white wine of the Veneto region of northwest Italy, is in fashion. British drinkers get through one out of every twelve bottles exported (twice the quantity consumed just five years previously), and the US does the same. Sales to Germany and Switzerland still account for half of all exports, but demand in these traditional markets is in decline.

Now that English-speaking markets have acquired a taste for Prosecco, serious producers are worried that the boom is backfiring. They gave a less than sparkling welcome to the launch in 2006 of Rich Prosecco, a canned version of the wine under the ineffable brand of Paris Hilton. 'It's yummy,' the socialite declared at the glitzy launch party in the Tyrol mountains. For a subsequent promotion, she was photographed naked except for a coat of gold paint, which matched the colour on the can.

Fulvio Brunetta, president of the Treviso wine growers association, whose members account for most of the production of Prosecco, was not minded to be gallant. 'Hilton hotels are a symbol of quality,' he said. 'Paris Hilton is not.'

COMPETITIVE EDGE

Years ago, I entered a competition in the *Observer* newspaper sponsored by Victoria Wine, Britain's first great high street wine merchant. The prize was alluring – the winner's own weight in Château Latour. At the time, Victoria Wine was part of Allied Lyons, a huge company that also owned a stake in the famed Pauillac *Premier Grand Cru Classé*. Some of the shops even sold the wine. Those were the days.

There was an elimination round and I was lucky enough to be among the half-dozen finalists called to a tasting competition, compèred by the great food and drink journalist Derek Cooper, in the firm's London cellars. I came third, and got a consolation prize, with which I was quite content. The winner was a decent sort of cove, an accountant I believe, and looked very happy on the huge weighing scale in the cellars as the cases of Latour were piled on the other side.

Lately, conscious of my own weight – I have ballooned perilously close to 13 stone – I have recalled this occasion, and idly wondered what I would be worth in Latour poundage. One bottle weighs just under 3lbs, and a case about 38lbs. I therefore tip the scale at five cases. I think the 2000 vintage would suit me, and at the current (2009) retail price, that values me at £50,000 in Latour. No wonder that accountant looked so smug.

A HEALTHY INVESTMENT

Christian Seely runs AXA Millésimes, a division of a very

large French insurance company which has successfully invested in several leading wine estates including the Bordeaux *Grand Cru Classé* Château Pichon-Longueville Baron. He likes to point out that the man after whom the estate is named, Baron Joseph de Pichon Longueville, lived a long life – he died aged 90 in 1850 – but that this was not exceptional for vineyard owners in the eighteenth and nineteenth centuries, even though average life expectancy in France was then only about 40 years.

'It is of course probable that the health-preserving qualities of regular consumption of his product was one of the factors in this phenomenon,' says Seely, 'but I think in fact there is more to it than that. When you spend your life looking after a few rows of vines, you are in close daily contact with the elemental forces of nature, and in a far more interesting way than if you were cultivating vegetables, since the unique character of every year can be distinctly expressed in the wine that you produce. It is endlessly fascinating, and worth staying alive for, to see what the next year will bring, and to follow the development of previous years' wines as they age in the bottle. Counting the interest on your money in the bank just has nothing on it.

'You will fall in love with your row of vines, and this is healthy. If you fall in love with your money in the bank, this is not. You will spend your life looking after your vines, and devoting yourself to understanding the land and the weather, which will mean something important to you every day. You will have the fascination as time goes by, of reviewing the essence of each year in the vineyard, preserved but constantly developing in the bottle. You will probably drink quite a lot of wine, have a lot of fun and meet a lot of great people. And on top of all this, it can be, if you do get it right, rather a good investment.'

WILD SPECULATION

The directors of London wine merchant Berry Bros. & Rudd, established in 1698, felt sufficiently confident on the firm's 310th anniversary to make some predictions for 50 years ahead, 2058. 'Rising global demand for fine wines – both for investment and for drinking – and limited availability of First Growth wines from top châteaux means prices will continue to rise inexorably over the next 50 years until fine wines become the preserve of the very rich,' they intoned, as if what they were forecasting had not already happened, which it has.

Berrys believes, by 2058, global bidding wars will take place for the top wines and the most sought-after wines will become prohibitively expensive and extremely difficult to obtain. This, combined with burgeoning interest in fine wine in Asia, South America, Central and Eastern Europe and Russia, will create a market so competitive that bidding wars for the few cases of highly praised, limited production wines will be common and a case of wine from a great vintage could cost £10 million.

It looks like a severe case of talking up the market, especially as Berry Bros. & Rudd is one of the leading retailers of precisely the sort of wines being talked about. But given that the supply of these wines is fixed and that there is no particular reason to anticipate a long-term fall in demand for them, there could just be something in it.

Simon Staples, the director in charge of fine wines, gave a particular example: 'If values increase by 15 per cent per annum as they have been doing recently, a case of 2005 Ch. Lafite-Rothschild, currently available for £9,200, could be worth just shy of £10 million by 2058.'

By the end of 2008, this notion was already sounding fanciful. Worldwide recession badly dented auction prices for first-growth wines and even Lafite '05 itself was found on sale in branches of French supermarket Carrefour at 650 euros per bottle, equating to a mere £7,000 or so per case. But Berrys held their ground, and in the spring of 2009 were listing the wine at £978 per bottle.

On a historic basis, the firm might still be vindicated. Take the vintage of 50 years earlier, the excellent 1955. Merchants like Berrys were selling the Lafite at about £20 a case when it first came on the market. Today, this wine is very scarce and a typical price from dealers in antique wines is £600 a bottle. An intact case would be a great rarity if it existed, and with good provenance might make, say, £10,000. That's 500 times the price of 50 years ago. If Berrys' Lafite 2005 appreciated at the same rate (assuming, of course, that the present downturn is not extravagantly worse that those of the 1970s and 1990s) it would be worth £4.6 million in 2058, under half of Simon Staples' proposed price, but still a decent long-term investment.

The usual provisos apply. The first is on the supply side. Lafite '55 is so rare now simply because most of it was consumed long ago. It was a low average for quantity, about 15,000 cases, but more significantly the vintage pre-dates the wine-investment era of the late 1960s. The people who bought '55s did so with the intention of drinking them, not speculating in them.

Now, it's very different. A large proportion of first-growth claret is bought by speculators. Much of the top wine from rated vintages such as 2005 will still be in storage, in original cases, 50 years hence as future generations of profiteers seek to enrich themselves. It's not a very appealing prospect for wine lovers, but for the owners of estates such as Lafite, who will escalate prices for successive harvests in accordance with market rates, it anticipates individual vintages that could net £200 billion, all from a vineyard of less than 250 acres.

IMPERFECT WORLD

Château Musar is an extraordinary enterprise. The château is indeed a castle, built in the seventeenth century at Ghazir on the Mediterranean, 15 miles north of Beirut, the capital of Lebanon. The vineyards are 30 miles or so inland in the Bekaa Valley. Musar is by no means the only active wine estate in the Lebanon, but it is the best known by a long shot, and considered by many merchants and critics to be one of the best and most distinctive producers in the world.

I have tasted the principal red wine many times, and have never ceased to be perplexed by its popularity. Labelled simply Château Musar, it is made from a blend of the kind of grapes you get in south-west France, Cabernet Sauvignon, Carignan, Cinsaut, Grenache, Mourvèdre. The finished product is a bold, vigorous and intense wine that tends to smell, disorientatingly, like cold tea and to exhibit volatility in the flavour. But it's made by a brave man, Serge Hochar. During Lebanon's civil war of the 1980s, the vineyards were the scene of fire fights, the Israelis used the place as a tank park and both the winery and the Hochar family home were shelled. The cellars in the castle have regularly served as an air-raid shelter.

Lebanon is in a period of peace, however uneasy, and Musar deserves to prosper. Serge Hochar freely admits his wine is quirky. 'I once produced a wine that was technically perfect,' he says, 'but it lacked the charms of imperfection.'

Europe produces two-thirds of all the world's wine. Millions of people are employed in the business, billions of bottles are made and consumed, and enormous bureaucracies regulate production and distribution. Laws are labyrinthine, enforcement rigorous. Wines that pretend to quality have to be made in closely defined locations and must come from specified grape varieties cultivated in strictly designated conditions. The quantity of grapes that can be harvested is subject to a maximum per hectare, and alcohol levels are subject to a minimum by volume.

It's a nightmare. Meanwhile, competing winemakers in nations such as Australia, the Americas and South Africa can do more or less what they like. The unintended consequence of this regulatory gulf is, of course, that wine frauds are almost exclusively European. Take the continuing action between the government of Italy and one of the nation's oldest winemaking dynasties. In allegations that first arose as long ago as 2005, the state claims Marchesi di Frescobaldi, a family firm which has been making wine in Tuscany for 700 years, has been exceeding the permitted quota of wine that can be brought in from outside the province to use for blending. As well as famous and expensive Chiantis, Frescobaldi also produces comparatively humble Indicazione Geografica Tipica wines. A bit like France's *vins de pays*, these can qualify as I.G.T. wines of Tuscany provided at least 85 per cent of the grapes are from the region. The balance of the fruit can come from elsewhere, perhaps to save a bit of money, or to enhance the blend. Fruit from Puglia, where Frescobaldi does get supplies, makes darker and more alcoholic wine, being from the broiling south, than the delicate stuff from the cooler, wetter vineyards of Tuscany. At the time of writing this book, the case was still pending. Frescobaldi denied exceeding any quota, refused an out-of-court deal with the authorities and opted for trial. The outcome was awaited with apprehension.

In Australia, they must view all this with disbelief. Down Under, there is no statutory differentiation between wines of this or that alleged quality. Yes, there are plenty of small-scale producers making wines entirely from their own grape harvests, but the big brands that compete in world markets with the likes of Frescobaldi's I.G.T. wines can truck the grapes halfway across the continent, or even buy in blending wine from the other side of the planet, if they feel like it. Regional typicity is strictly an old world concept.

It all seems terribly unfair, but the likelihood of deregulation in Europe is zilch. The rules that govern production, such as the Denominazione di Origine Controllata of Italy, the Appellation d'Origine Contrôlée of France and the bogglingly complex Qualitätswein standards of Germany were hard won in the first half of the last century, and unravelling them could serve no one's interests. And even during the currency of these laws, there have been some spectacular breaches along the way.

LETHAL DOSE

The most pernicious of all wine scandals was the Italian methanol outrage of 1986. Early in the year, a number of suspicious deaths in the Milan area were attributed to poisoning from methyl alcohol or methanol, a solvent used in industrial processes, and of renowned toxicity. A dose of 10ml, enough to fill an eggcup, can cause permanent blindness; 30ml can be fatal.

Post-mortem evidence revealed at least 23 victims, and that all had recently drunk wine. How many others lost their eyesight, suffered the other terrible consequences of methanol poisoning or died undiagnosed will never be known. The police did rapidly trace the sources – to a large number of producers, bottlers and merchants – and the picture emerged. Vast quantities of wine had been adulterated in a scam intended to defraud the European Union (then the EEC), which under the Common Agriculture Policy bought excess production in order to support grape growers unable to find a market. All the fraudsters had to do was to produce liquid with sufficient alcohol to qualify, and doctoring worthless wine with methanol was the cheapest way to bring it to the required level. Methanol had not always been so affordable, but new legislation had just abolished the excise duty previously levied on it, on the grimly ironic grounds that it was not drinkable. According to later testimony, as much as 260 tonnes of methanol had been mixed with wine, enough to kill 85 million people.

The intention of the adulterators was, obviously enough, simply to swindle money out of Brussels. The eurocrats would dispatch the wine for distilling for industrial use. No one would be harmed. But in the way of these things, other criminals became involved. They reckoned they could pass the wine off. Some of it was even exported, to France and Germany, but in neither of those countries did it get past the quality inspectors. Many lives were undoubtedly saved.

All the known victims were Italian. The nation's wine industry took years to recover from the suspicion and disgrace, particularly in key export markets such as the United States. In the European Parliament, British farming spokeswoman Barbara Castle roundly blamed the Common Agricultural Policy, and did not spare Italian feelings: 'The drawback of the CAP is that prices are fixed centrally, and to keep the least economic chap in production. But monitoring for quality is done nationally, and in Italy it is not the acme.'

VIN DE PAYS D'OCTORED?

Early in 2009, a regional newspaper in France's Languedoc region, *La Dépêche*, reported that Carcassonne police had been alerted to an anomaly in the local wine-export figures. In the preceding three years, sales overseas of Pinot Noir reds made under the regional vin de pays d'Oc designation were recorded at 160 million bottles. But the annual production of Pinot Noir wines from the entire region was only 67 million bottles. Pinot Noir vin de pays wines typically sell for twice the price of reds from other grape varieties, and Pinot Noir brands have been enjoying marked success on the American market. Investigations have begun both locally and in the US.

EXTENDED VINTAGE

David Molyneux-Berry, former wine auctioneer, recalled to a conference in California in 2007 that a late owner of Château Lafleur in Pomerol had told him he had produced only five magnums of the superb 1947 vintage. Molyneux-Berry was therefore perplexed to know that at least 18 magnums of the same wine had been sold at auction since 2004. He conceded that some of the wine was sold in cask to merchants at home and abroad, but given the small production (only about 40 barriques, equal to 12,000 bottles in all) it seemed unlikely so much wine in an unusual bottle size would still be extant 60 years after the vintage.

DRESSED AS MOUTON

Serena Sutcliffe, head of Sotheby's wine department, acknowledged in 2008 that counterfeiting is a problem in the USA and Asia, where European fraudsters are taking advantage of wealthy enthusiasts who know little more about the most desirable wines than their names and would be unlikely to spot a fake. Ms Sutcliffe recalled a case of wine submitted for sale, purporting to be Château Mouton Rothschild 1982. 'The original wooden case looked perfect, each bottle was wrapped in what looked like original paper. We pulled the cork and it was hardly impregnated by the wine at all. It wasn't Mouton and it wasn't 1982.'

BAD YEAR IN BEAUJOLAIS

Georges Duboeuf, the veteran 'King of Beaujolais', had an off year in 2006. His company, the largest producer in the region, was fined by a French court for blending wines of differing quality designations from the 2004 vintage. It was an attempt, the prosecution alleged, to pass off inferior wines under labels for which they did not qualify. The production manager responsible was fined, given a three-month suspended prison sentence and resigned from his job. Duboeuf, born 1933, pleaded that he had not known of the incident, and pointed out that none of the wine concerned had even been bottled, let alone offered on the market.

Beaujolais has not had a good run. In 2003 a group of producers brought an action for defamation against a magazine published in the region, *Lyon Mag*, over an article quoting a leading expert's view that quite a lot of Beaujolais wine was *vin de merde*. A court in Villefranche, at the heart of the vineyard region, found for the plaintiffs and fined *Lyon Mag* €284,143, sufficient to bankrupt it. But the producers' triumph was to wither on the vine. National newspapers in France, led by *Le Monde*, and then around the world, picked up the story and ridiculed the judgement. Funds were raised to finance an appeal – Britain's Circle of Wine Writers contributed a princely sum – and in 2005 at France's appeal court, the ruling was overturned. The producers were ordered to pay €2,000 towards the magazine's court costs, but the loss to the good name of Beaujolais remains beyond estimation.

A Sniff of History

The greatest wine robbery in history took place on 29 April 1587. It was the day Sir Francis Drake sailed into the port of Cadiz, Spain, with a naval squadron of 24 ships intent on destroying the invasion fleet, or armada, then in preparation in the harbour. In the action, later celebrated as the 'singeing of the King of Spain's beard', Drake's crews boarded 32 Spanish warships, many still under construction, stripped them of all movables and then either burned them or sailed them away, loaded with the mountainous booty.

The raiders faced determined, if utterly confused, resistance from the Cadiz garrison, but this did not deter Drake from seizing what he found on the dockside. Awaiting shipment were 2,900 butts of sack (the precursor of sherry). Although he knew the garrison would be reinforced by a large detachment of troops marching from Seville within a short time, Drake insisted on loading the entire cargo – each 500-litre butt weighed about a ton – aboard his captured ships. It took three days.

Safely shipped back to England, where the wine was auctioned in the London docks at premium prices, this enormous prize made Drake rich and his sponsor, Queen Elizabeth I, several times richer. The loss to the Spanish wine trade was immense – the booty represented a tenth of an entire year's peacetime exports – but demand for the looted sack, so dramatically stolen from under King Philip II's nose, boosted sales of the wine in England for decades to come.

THE CREATION OF CHIANTI

Chianti is the classic Italian wine, and has a classically Italian legend attached to its origins. The story concerns a serious-minded Florentine landowner and agricultural pioneer, Baron Bettino Ricasoli, who became the second prime minister of newly united Italy in 1861.

The story goes something like this. When just married, young Bettino took his bride, Anna Bonacorssi, to a society ball in Florence. Known derisively as il Barone de Ferro, the Iron Baron, because of his unbending moral uprightness, the groom lived up to his nickname on this occasion when he learned that a dashing young man at the ball had had a dance too many with the beautiful Anna.

By no means a handsome figure himself, and jealous in the way that only an Italian knows how, Bettino took umbrage. He angrily summoned his carriage and conveyed *la bella signora* through the night to the gloomy family seat, Castello Brolio, far away in the Chianti hills of the Tuscan hinterland.

There, the baroness was to languish for the rest of her days, far from the temptations of libertine Florence society. She was, of course, attentively watched over by her green-eyed protector, who beguiled the many wilderness years of his political life in his vineyards, devising what we now call Chianti wine.

Ricasoli's artful blend of grape varieties, mostly Sangiovese, Canaiolo and Colorino, remained the formula for Chianti for more than a century and the wine continues to owe its essential character to his experiments in the Brolio vineyards, which have reputedly been in production since 1141. Ricasoli remains a leading player within the Chianti Classico zone, marketing its *riserva* wines under the name Brolio. And in charge today is the present Baron, Francesco, great-great-great grandson of old jellybags himself.

THRICE RECOMMENDED

The first really odd wine name is probably Est! Est!! Est!!! It perpetuates a medieval tale concerning Bishop Johannes Fugger of Augsburg. He was travelling from his Bavarian see to Rome in 1111 to attend the coronation of the Emperor Henry V, and on each day of the long journey sent his faithful servant Martin ahead to scout for the inns with the best wines. When Martin found one, he was on orders to chalk 'Est!' on the door, so his master would know he could enter with confidence. The word was merely an abbreviated code for *vinum est bonum*, the wine is good.

At Montefiascone, about 100 miles short of Rome, Martin found an inn with a wine of transcending quality. He wished the Bishop to be in no doubt, and wrote Est! Est!! Est!!! on the door. Fugger was more than impressed, he was converted. He could not tear himself away from the wine and his journey ended there in Montefiascone, where he is buried at the church of San Flavio. His epitaph, said to have been written by Martin, blamed his expiry on an excess of the wine, but this did not deter Montefiascone from adopting the name that commemorates the legend.

WHAT'S YOUR POISON?

Wines today are made with added sugar, acids, sulphur, diammonium phosphate and other chemicals. Many are fermented with genetically modified yeasts and clarified with beef or fish gelatin, or a clay called bentonite. Some wines are pasteurized. It's all entirely legal under even the strictest regulations, such as those prevailing in the European Union and the United States.

But it is a major improvement on the past. Dangerous additives go back to Roman times, when lead was used in wine – and in countless other food and drink products – as a preservative and sweetener. It was only in the 1690s that the lethal nature of lead came to light thanks to a German doctor, Eberhard Gockel. He was physician to a number of monasteries at Ulm in the Württemberg vineyard region, and observed that the monks who drank the most wine were the likeliest to suffer a painful colic disorder that frequently developed into paralysis and blindness. Many patients died. Gockel recognized these symptoms as similar to those experienced by lead miners and pottery workers in Saxony, whose epidemic suffering had been noted in the medical literature some years earlier. Gockel asked the supplier of the wine to the monasteries to desist from using lead, and the monks showed a marked improvement.

In 1696, the Duke of Württemberg issued an edict making it a capital crime to adulterate wine with lead. It was the first health-based consumer-protection legislation of its kind, and proved understandably efficacious.

MONTE CHRISTO PISTOLS

Macon in Georgia, USA, was the scene of one of the first great newspaper hoaxes. The victim was not an American paper, but *The Times* of London, which in 1856 received, believed and published a report from an Englishman, John Arrowsmith, who claimed to have travelled aboard a train bound from Macon to Augusta on which several passengers appeared to have died. The fatalities were the consequence of a succession of duels fought with 'Monte Christo pistols', alleged the report. The train had stopped six times along the 120-mile route, it was claimed, so

that passengers thus armed could disembark and discharge these weapons at each other.

It was several weeks before *The Times* discovered that a Monte Christo pistol was a bottle of champagne in Dixie slang, and that a dead man was common slang for an empty bottle.

A TREMENDOUS REPORT

An edited fragment from the journal of a Royalist gentleman, Gerald Grinling of Cirencester, Gloucestershire, entered 24 January 1661:

A near-catastrophe in the cellar. Last week my friend Kenelm Digby arrived with a collection of his new bottles. They are thick-lipped glass vessels of muddy hue and filled with a substance he asserts will emerge in a condition of Effervescence when the bungs, which are tied on to the neck with stout twine as if they might try to escape the bottle under their own will, are drawn.

'The secret of the liveliness lies in the second fermentation,' Digby told me, oblivious to the Perplexity that is ever plain on my face when he discourses on his strange Alchemies. 'A wiping of yeast around the bung, which is then flogged fully into the neck and in three or four days you will have a remarkable surprise.'

Today, I was taking stock with Coolthirst of the cellars, which have been quite perturbingly depleted during the recent celebrations to mark the Restoration of our Most Gracious Sovereign King Charles. Just as my unfortunate *major domo* had made his way down the steps, there came a Tremendous Report from beneath my feet, followed at once by a crash of glass and a Frightful Shriek.

I rushed to the hatch, to see Coolthirst spread-eagled immediately below, clutching at his breeches and bleeding profusely on to the floor. I hauled the wretch up the steps, fearing the Worst. But having got past him to my precious store of bottled Vins I found them mercifully untouched. Save, that is, for one of Digby's infernal inventions, which, presumably from the exigencies of the yeast, had blown itself into the Smithereens now to be found embedded into casks and tuns in every quarter of the cellars.

Instructed Coolthirst, who has not borne this incident gladly, to have Cook extract the several shards quite plainly projecting from his person and then to remove the remaining bombs from the cellars forthwith. Note to inform Digby that his notion of enlivened wine clearly has no future whatsoever.

KARL MARX'S FAMILY VINEYARDS

The family of Karl Marx, who was born at Trier in Germany's Mosel region in 1818, owned vineyards nearby at Mertesdorf on the river Ruwer. At an early age, Karl became aware of the plight of winemakers in the region, burdened by poor prices and punitive taxes, on top of a bad run of vintages from 1840. In the press, he attacked the Prussian authorities' alleged indifference to the region's interests, and these reports contributed to his forced exile.

While living beyond his means in London and Paris, Marx was notorious for pleading for money from home. He hoped to inherit the vineyards, but never did. The family sold them in 1857.

The Weiss family of the Erben von Buelwitz estate produces a Karl Marx Spätburgunder (Pinot Noir) wine from their vineyard, close to the Marxes' former property in honour of the great man. This is, uncommonly for the region but appropriately for the association, a red wine.

AS LAID DOWN

H. Warner Allen recalled in his classic work *Sherry and Port* one of his own ancestors, a Mayor of Rye who was 'greatly addicted to Port'. Late in life, he took to his bed. His manservant explained to a visitor how he nursed the master: 'I keeps a-turning his Worship, 'cause you see, sir, he's got that much Port in his inside, he'd be bound to get crusted, if I let 'un stop too long on one side.'

PORT BENEFITS FROM FRAUD

It was common practice until the last century for British wine merchants to import burgundy and claret, port and sherry in casks, pay the duty and then covertly extend the contents of each cask by adding quantities of home-made 'wine' fermented from imported grape must (non-dutiable), from raisins or any other sugar-bearing material that came to hand.

Producers could be equally untrustworthy. In the eighteenth century, the boom in port sales that followed the Methuen Treaty of 1703, slashing English taxes on Portuguese imports at a time of punitive duties on French wines, stretched the capacity of the Douro Valley grape growers beyond breaking point. Annual shipments grew from a few hundred pipes (each of 700 bottles) to 20,000 by 1750, and vineyard planting could not keep up. Farmers resorted to adding *baga*, the juice of elderberries that grew in profusion in the region. The drawback was that the wine, darkened and intensified by this foreign matter, tasted revolting. Drinkers in Britain – the sole market for port – complained. Sales crashed. The shippers had to take action.

In 1755, the British Association in Oporto, representing the interests of the 'factors' – agents for London wine shippers – combined to cut the price offered farmers for a pipe from a usual £10 to just £2. Perhaps the British had anticipated what the farmers would do: turn to the Portuguese government, pleading imminent ruin. The factors knew that the prime minister, the Marquis of Pombal, disliked their monopoly of the port trade. And again they might have foreseen what Pombal ordered: the formation of the Alto Douro Wine Company which, in the manner of a nationalized marketing board, would purchase all the farmers' wine. The shippers must buy from the company at take-it-or-leave-it prices.

But now it became the company's task to ensure that the wine was fit for sale. While the factors had no powers to enforce quality standards on the farmers, the Portuguese state most certainly did. Growers trying to pass off *baga* as the real thing faced severe punishment. Pombal insisted that all elder plants in the region be destroyed. He decided that wines destined for the factors, and thus for export, should come only from the part of the region with the best vineyards – an area designated the Factory Zone.

Prices, of course, went up. But so did quality. It was from this time that port won its reputation as a quality product, so much so that it became known as 'the Englishman's wine'. Naturally, the farmers tried to cheat the Company, and less scrupulous shippers carried on swindling their customers in Britain by stretching the port before bottling. But an industry that became a mainstay of the Portuguese economy for more than two centuries, and an indispensable comfort to millions of drinkers worldwide, had taken root.

THE MAKING OF MADEIRA

Madeira wine owes its continuing existence to a royal whim. In 1663, Charles II declared that all exports carried from anywhere in Europe to his American colonies must be carried on 'British bottoms' – English ships.

Overnight, this decree killed off the legal wine trade between the prosperous and thirsty settlers of New England and the Carolinas and their well-established wine suppliers in France and Spain. But Madeira was exempted. Although Portuguese-owned since its discovery by Henry the Navigator in the previous century, the fact that the island was definitely not European – it is 300 miles offshore west of Casablanca – permitted ships of any flag to carry its wines to the Americas.

Madeira, then a straightforward table wine, had not hitherto enjoyed much reputation, but now it became the tipple of choice in British America. It was at this time that the custom began of distilling some of the wine and adding it to the barrels to boost its stability, strength and longevity – a change in style tailor-made for robust American tastes.

And it was on the long Atlantic crossings that Madeira shippers discovered their wines actually improved by being exposed to heat in the butts (casks) on or below decks. In time, Madeira producers started to replicate this effect by heating the wines in the sun or by other means – as they still do today.

FLYING THE FLAG IN MARSALA

Even though Sicily's winemaking traditions date back millennia, the island's most famous sweet wine lacks ancient, or even strictly indigenous, provenance. Marsala is a confection created as recently as 1773 by Liverpool-born John Woodhouse, who exploited the island's underdeveloped vineyards, and underemployed population, to make wines that would rival costlier port and Malaga, then in great demand in England. The wine takes its name from Marsala, the seaport at the island's westernmost point.

Woodhouse was fortunate in the timing of the Napoleonic Wars. French occupation of Italy drove the King of Naples into exile in Sicily, where he received the support of a large British garrison, fortified by the presence of Admiral Nelson's Mediterranean fleet. The Royal Navy stocked its ships with Marsala in place of rum and the drink consequently enjoyed loyal popularity in Britain. It soon became the principal export of western Sicily. The port became a British *entrepôt* comparable with Vila Nova de Gaia in Portugal. It continued a long tradition of British presence here. The 16 great grey marble columns of the town's basilica, for example, were destined for Canterbury Cathedral, but were salvaged from the ship which, bound for England, foundered off Marsala in the thirteenth century.

Marsala, formerly Lilybaeum, was the principal stronghold of Carthage in Sicily until it was surrendered to the Romans in 241 BC at the conclusion of the First Punic War. The origin of the present name is Saracen, from Marsa Ali, port of Ali. Garibaldi began his campaign at Marsala when he landed there with 1,000 men in 1860.

Under quality regulations of 1984 basic Marsala wine is fortified with *cotto*, a caramelized grape syrup, and grape spirit to make two styles: Fine, aged four months or more at a minimum 17 per cent alcohol (formerly called Italy Particular or IP); Superiore, aged two years at a minimum 18 per cent alcohol (formerly Superior Old Marsala or SOM, London Particular or LP and Garibaldi Dolce or GD). Vergine and Vergine Stravecchio are different, usually unfortified and reaching the required 18 per cent alcohol through evaporation during long ageing (minimum five and ten years respectively) in cask.

'Cooking' Marsala, especially for zabaglione dessert, with added egg, or flavoured with the likes of banana, chocolate and coffee, seriously diminished connoisseurs' interest in the authentic wine, prompting new regulations in 1969 as well as 1984. Under these, the culinary brands are now labelled 'Cremoso Zabaione Vino Aromatizzato' or annotated *'preparato con l'Impiego di vino* Marsala'.

EXCESS DUTY

Like many bad things, the Romans started it. The *vectigal rerum venalium* was the original excise duty, originally levied in the first century BC, on goods sold in open markets in Rome. It was introduced by Augustus at 1 per cent (*centesima*) of value, halved by Tiberius and finally abolished, in AD 38, by Caligula. It was, in common with all such taxes, imposed to fund the gross excesses of government.

Excise did not stage a comeback for 16 centuries. No monarch even of the Middle Ages seems to have dared try it. But when the Puritan-dominated Parliament in Britain seized fiscal power from King Charles I during the English Civil War, it was quick to consider the tax.

The regime of the day was, as ever since, reticent about its intentions. This is a government statement of 1641: 'The Houses of Parliament, receiving information that divers public rumours and aspersions are by malignant persons cast upon this house, that they intend to assess every man's pewter and lay Excise upon that and other commodities, the said House, for their vindication do declare these rumours are false and scandalous.'

The first Excise Ordinance was duly introduced two years later for 'the speedy raising and levying of monies for the maintenance of the forces raising by Parliament' and, of course, 'only for the duration of the war'.

The method of collection was inspired by the indirect taxation levied in Holland, where to finance a burgeoning navy, the state collected percentages of the value of alcoholic drinks. In Britain, the tax was extended to beer, meat, clothes, leather and salt. Further money-spinning schemes were added. Fees were demanded for issuing licences to sell game, medicines, imported wines and snuff. Pawnbrokers, pedlars, auctioneers and other riff-raff were also required to buy a licence if they wished to continue their trades.

To enforce it all, Excise Commissioners were appointed. The original eight nominees worked on a commission of 3d in every £1 collected – or 1¼ per cent. The commissioners and their officers had almost unlimited powers when it came to collections – including the right of entry and search into the homes of citizens. Overnight, this ended one of the most basic privileges of British life – the inviolability of private homes.

The excise, the first tax ever to be levied on ordinary working people, was spectacularly unpopular, and evaded on an epic scale. Excise officers were resisted, attacked and occasionally murdered. The army was regularly called out to assist with enforcement. For all that, collecting was profitable work, with generous salaries offered, and ample scope for corruption.

When Cromwell's Commonwealth (euphemism for Republic) came to its inevitable end in 1660 and the Crown was restored, it was widely anticipated that the new levies would be revoked. But King Charles II was not a man to overlook a source of ready income. Within his first year in power, the excise had been increased not only on alcoholic drinks, but extended to tea, coffee and chocolate. The proceeds, which went to the Crown, amounted to about £250,000 a year – uncountable millions at today's values.

Alongside customs duties, levied on imports since the Middle Ages, the revenue from excise funded the greater part of public expenditure in Britain until the twentieth century. The idea of taxing income – 'direct' tax – did not occur to politicians until the blackest days of the Napoleonic Wars, when Parliament again felt the need to introduce a temporary levy, in addition, of course, to hugely increased excise duties on alcohol and on luxuries such as bricks, glass, soap, salt and candles.

In 2008, Britain took over from the Republic of Ireland at the top of the wine-excise league when duty per 75cl bottle was raised first to £1.46, then to £1.53 and, in 2009, to £1.60. Among European Union nations, only Ireland, Sweden and Finland levy duty above £1 and the next harshest regime is Denmark's at 42p. France levies 2p, and 15 of the 27 member countries, including Italy, Austria, Germany, Greece, Portugal and Spain, levy none at all.

PRIME THIRST

There is a fine tradition in British politics of overlooking national disagreements in the interests of maintaining a decent supply of wine. Take Robert Walpole, appointed the first 'prime minister' in 1715 by George I. The King spoke no English and could not participate in the proceedings of parliament. He trusted Walpole sufficiently to make him the premier instrument of his government, even though he must have known very well what the MP had been up to under the previous regime of Queen Anne.

Walpole had been Secretary of War and Treasurer to the Royal Navy. During the War of the Spanish Succession, as British forces clashed with the *grandes armées* of Louis XIV and trade with France was outlawed, Walpole persistently breached his own government's embargo by smuggling in huge quantities of claret and champagne for his private cellar. On one occasion, he prevailed on an official to commandeer a naval launch to carry a cargo of illicit casks up the Thames to his London home, bribing the customs men along the way.

Among Walpole's favourite French wines was Château Margaux. The estate's records show that the prime minister was in the habit of ordering four casks, equivalent to 1,200 bottles, every three months, but that he did not always pay for them.

GENEROUS HELPINGS

Horace Walpole in 1755 recorded the benefits of a diet including plenty of port. Lord Fitzwalter, he wrote, sustained himself through the last months of his life, in his eighty-fifth year, with a daily diet of two barrels of oysters, three bottles of port and a bottle of brandy.

In 1779, publisher George Selwyn told of Dr Warner's dinner party. The host and his two guests drank a bottle of hock, then one of port, with the meal. They followed with two bottles of claret, then two of burgundy, and finished with a bottle of cherry brandy.

NO FEAR OF SLURS

Drunkenness was not stigmatized in public life in the eighteenth century in the way it is today. Members of Parliament often required assistance to remain upright while making speeches in the House, but at little or no risk of comment in the press. And the statesmen of the day knew how to hold their drink. This is Macaulay on Pitt, who rationed himself to six bottles of port a day during most of his 20-odd years as Prime Minister:

> He indulged too freely in wine but it was very seldom that any indication of undue excess could be detected in his tones or gestures; and in truth, two bottles of port will be little more to him than two dishes of tea.

FRONT MAN

George Sandeman, founder in 1790 of the great port house, made heroic efforts to maintain supplies of wines to British officers during the Napoleonic Wars. He frequently visited the front line and made deliveries wherever they were requested. A letter from Colonel Bryan O'Toole written to Sandeman on 5 January 1815, demonstrates just how much this was appreciated:

Your so kindly remembering the cold uncomfortable quarters I gave you is a thorough proof of the goodness of your heart. Colonel Prior forwarded to me your pipe of port, which is the best I ever drank. It arrived in pudding time, just before Christmas, when I had a dozen of friends to keep the holidays with me, and they found it so good that I could hardly get them out of the house yesterday. Your health, my good sir, was drank with three cheers in a bumper of it every day after our cheese.

NAPOLEONIC CHAMPAGNE

There is a touching story of Napoleon Bonaparte's last campaign before his abdication of 1814. Refusing peace even after the catastrophic retreat from Moscow, the Emperor cavalierly submitted France to invasion by the Russians, whose Cossacks overran and ravaged Champagne, trapping Bonaparte in Epernay. There, he billeted himself with Jean-Rémy Moët of the celebrated champagne *maison*. The two had been friends for many years, and in gratitude for his loyalty (and perhaps in contrition for the needless destruction he had visited on Champagne) Napoleon solemnly rewarded Moët with the Légion d'Honneur, the order Bonaparte had himself inaugurated in 1802. This was no ordinary gesture, for the cross and ribbon he pinned to his friend's chest was his own.

It was an act of kindness and humility not entirely in keeping with the character of the man who brought France a decade of imperial grandeur at a cost of one and a half million French lives, as well as incalculable destruction to his enemies. But France forgave Napoleon, and chooses to remember *La Gloire* rather than *le chagrin*. Champagne, which had been a battlefield long before 1814 and has seen worse since, has positively taken Napoleon to its bosom. Moët & Chandon commemorate the great man in the name of their Brut Impérial non-vintage wine, tactfully renamed Première Cuvée for the British market.

In one sense, the champagne producers as a whole had reason to be grateful to Napoleon for the nemesis of 1814, because the Russian officers who swept into the vineyards and cellars of Epernay and Reims were thus introduced to the delights of the extraordinary sparkling wines made there. Naturally, they helped themselves, but their occupation was a brief one, and their thirst eternal. Nicole-Barbe Ponsardin Clicquot, better known as La Veuve Clicquot, watched with equanimity as her cellars were looted. 'They drink today,' she said, 'but tomorrow they'll pay.' She was as good as her word. Following Napoleon's abdication, the occupiers withdrew, and Mme Clicquot immediately sent her salesman, with a shipload of samples, to Russia. In the triumphal mood prevailing there, sales were brisk indeed, and the market that was to make champagne the vast business it is today was thereby created.

Napoleon himself was keenly appreciative of champagne. Throughout his campaigns, he had supplies of the wine carried along with the other impedimenta of his armies. Victories had to be celebrated, and representatives of the champagne houses were frequently to be found among the camp followers, eagerly awaiting the outcome of each battle in order to make timely approaches to the victorious side.

Several champagne houses claim that Napoleon showed a preference for their wines. Quite apart from the hospitality he received at Moët & Chandon, where they built a fine pavilion exclusively for his use (it still stands), the Emperor also stayed with the Ponsardin family in Reims, where no doubt he would have made the acquaintance of Clicquot wines.

The smaller *maison* of Jacquesson et Fils found imperial favour in 1810 when Napoleon visited their cellars in Chalons-sur-Marne and awarded the firm a gold medal for '*la beauté et la richesse de nos caves*'. Jacquesson have since moved to the charmingly named village of Dizy, but still proudly display the medal on their labels, and recall that Napoleon toasted his victory at Wagram with bottles of their wine.

NAPOLEON BRANDY

It is not only with champagne that Napoleon's name has associations. The cognac industry has long dressed itself in the Emperor's finery. The original 'Napoleon Brandy' is said to have been that of the great vintage year of 1811, bottled specially for the Emperor with the embossed 'N' on the neck. It seems improbable Napoleon would ever have encountered any of this spirit, as he had been exiled to St Helena before it would have been bottled. This has not forestalled a lively market for allegedly priceless bottles of this brandy which by now, of course, are collectable rather than drinkable. Most, no doubt, are fakes.

One cognac house, Courvoisier, has adopted Napoleon as an important symbol. There is a genuine association, for several casks of Courvoisier were loaded on to the frigate in which Bonaparte was supposed to escape to America after Waterloo. But the ship was intercepted by the British, and the cognac taken as a prize. Ever since, Courvoisier has produced a Napoleon brandy, as the term has also been adopted for any cognac which has had five or more years' barrel age before bottling. Unhappily for the name of the great man, the Napoleon-labelled spirits are not the best-quality bottles in the producers' ranges, but the second best. Thus is France's greatest soldier, law-giver and ego-maniac fondly commemorated.

CON MERCHANTS

German nobleman Hermann von Pückler-Muskau, touring England in 1826 in search of a suitable bride, noted the following in his diary while staying at the Travellers' Club in London:

> The fare, or rather the food, (the *raison d'être* for most of them and not a little important to me, too) is prepared mostly by Frenchmen, and is as good and wholesome as you will find anywhere in London.
>
> Since the Club buys its wines itself and sells them on at cost, they are cheap and very drinkable. But it is a peculiarity of the English that gourmets, even in the best families, seldom if ever secure the finest wines. They do not buy direct from the vineyards as we do, but insist upon letting wine merchants in London supply them. And what a venal trade that is – rife with malpractice and misrepresentation! Indeed the other day yet another merchant, brought before the Bench on a charge of avoiding the Duty on several thousand bottles of Claret and Port in his cellars, got off scot-free by pleading that he *produced* all of it here in London! So you may well imagine what they and their like must brew and pass off under the pretence of some well-known Champagne label, or even in the name of Lafitte.
>
> The merchants rarely acquire the very best wines from, for

example, the Fatherland, for the simple reason that they make barely a penny out of them. Or, at most, they buy in just enough to pour into their rubbish and render it passable.

BURIED TREASURE FROM THE SECOND WORLD WAR

Bordeaux wines made before the Second World War are now very rare. During the years of the conflict, most of the pre-war vintages stored in Britain were, understandably, consumed. In occupied France and elsewhere on the Continent, wines that were not looted by the Germans were no doubt drunk before they fell into the wrong hands.

But some wines were concealed. In 2009, London auctioneers Bonhams offered for sale an extraordinary collection of clarets that had been hidden from the Nazis on the island of Guernsey. Local merchants Bucktrout & Co. had moved these treasures into a window-less 'middle cellar' below the quayside premises in St Peter Port from which they had been trading since 1830. Although the harbour was bombed, with much loss of life, by the Luftwaffe on 28 June 1940 and all the Channel Islands were then occupied until May 1945, the wines survived intact. When Bucktrout & Co. finally moved to a new address – the firm is still very much in business – they decided to put the old wines up for sale. Included were Château Latour 1926, Châteaux Ausone and Mouton Rothschild 1928 and Château Margaux 1929. The wines fetched a modest total of £50,000.

ORDERLY LOOTERS

The Nazi occupation of France from 1940–45 was a melancholy chapter in the history of wine. Naturally, the Germans looted the wine everywhere they went. They made it difficult for the *vignerons* to carry on working by diverting vital materials. They halted normal trade. They requisitioned cellars as defence positions, billeted troops in the châteaux and turned vineyards into airstrips, artillery ranges, encampments.

But in the classic regions of France, the occupiers went about this in a systematic way. Berlin did not want the French wine industry simply destroyed. A continuing source of wine was needed for the enjoyment of Germans at home and abroad. In Bordeaux, a *weinführer* was appointed to oversee the (compulsory) purchase of wine for Germany, and to ensure discipline among the occupiers. No *bibliothèque* (collection of old vintages) escaped the looting, but few among the great estates lost more than part of the whole.

At Mouton-Rothschild, home to one of the world's greatest collections of old wines from countless châteaux, the cellars remained largely unscathed. This was partly because the Vichy government seized the property on the grounds it had been in Jewish ownership, which put it out of bounds to the Germans. But it was also because the *weinführer,* Heinz Bömers, insisted Mouton should be respected. Bömers had been a wine importer in Bremen before the war and was well acquainted with many of the Bordeaux producers. He was not a supporter of the Nazi Party, but as a prominent member of the German wine trade past the age for military service, he was a shoo-in for the job.

Heinz Bömers is still remembered by the old guard in Bordeaux as an autocratic figure but nevertheless a just one, given the circumstances. He had been the agent in Bremen for Mouton-Rothschild before the war, and afterwards, when the estate was returned to Baron Philippe de Rothschild, he reappointed him. Bömers continued in the role until his old age.

If You Really Want to Know

Still 'table' wine is made by cultivating grapes, picking them at an ideal ripeness, crushing them to liberate the juice, then fermenting it until all the natural sugar turns into alcohol. It's then just a matter of maturing, clarifying and bottling the finished product. There are plenty of variations, such as the perplexing malo-lactic fermentation, which is desirable in some wines, and not in others, and can be either stimulated or suppressed by the winemaker. Sparkling and fortified wines are made in their own mysterious ways. The basic methods for making still wines differ according to colour.

The red wine process:

1. Black-skinned (and occasionally white-skinned) grapes are fed into an auger, a screw-threaded contraption that strips the bunches off their stems and crushes the fruit.
2. The squashed fruit or 'must' is fed into a fermenting vat. The juice is clear in all grapes, so the colour – and compounds such as tannins – come from fermenting the juice along with its skins and pips.
3. A cultured yeast is added, and fermentation typically takes up to two weeks, turning the natural sugars in the fruit into alcohol, typically 12 to 14 per cent by volume.

4. The 'free-run' wine is piped to storage tanks and the skins and pips left behind are pressed to extract the remaining wine.

5. The vats of free-run and pressed wine might be blended together, or bottled separately as wines of differing quality. Cheaper wines are clarified and bottled about six months after the harvest. Others are matured in tanks or oak casks for varying periods, up to several years, before bottling.

The white wine process:

1. Grapes, usually white-skinned, are fed into a stemmer-crusher, which strips off the stems and crushes the fruit.

2. The fruit is fed into a press, which extracts the juice.

3. The juice only, without the skins, is piped into a fermenting vat. A cultured yeast is added. If the wine is to be dry, fermentation will continue for up to two weeks until the natural sugars become alcohol. Again, 12 to 14 per cent is usual. If the wine is to be 'medium' or sweet, the fermenting process is halted by killing the yeast, leaving a controlled residue of sugar.

4. The wine is piped into storage tanks to await blending, clarifying and bottling. White wines can be bottled just a few weeks after the vintage. Some are matured in oak casks.

The rosé wine process:

The process starts as for red wines but when the free-run juice has taken on the desired colour, it is piped off the skins into vats to complete fermentation. Some rosé is made simply by blending red and white wines.

WHY DO SWEET GRAPES MAKE DRY WINE?

Winemakers are impatient about answering stupid questions like this, but I once interviewed a chemist working in the industry, Colin Hamilton, who kindly offered this unusually lucid explanation:

Most of us instinctively profess a preference for dry wine. All reds should be dry, and just about all whites. But what *is* a dry wine? How does a drink made from sweet grapes get that way? The word to hang on to is acidity. This is the single most important determinant in the dryness of a wine. The acidity is, in effect, the measure of a wine's sharpness. It gives the wine its life. Without it, wine would lose its association with the fruit it is made from – because all fruits contain acid.

Grapes have two distinct kinds of acid, tartaric and malic. Tartaric may be familiar from the tartrates found in bottles and casks, salts of acid potassium which you find stuck to the wet side of a newly pulled cork. Malic (from Latin *malus*, apple) is the harsh acid in unripe grapes, making them taste as sour as green apples. The riper a grape is when it's picked, the more of the desirable tartaric acid it should contain, and the less sour malic. Tartaric acid is also associated with keeping potential, while malic is associated with wines which need to be consumed young.

Overall, the effect of acidity on the palate is to balance other elements of the wine, especially sugar and alcohol. If the acidity is too low, the wine tastes 'flabby' – a favourite wine taster's term which translates broadly as watery – and lacks freshness. If the acidity is too high, the wine tastes tart and out of balance.

Just to make it all more complicated, there are three more types of acidity significant in wine. One is succinic, an acid formed during primary fermentation. Two is lactic (yes, as in milk): malic acid is converted to this softer-tasting acid when a bacterial malolactic fermentation is allowed to take place in the wine. Three is acetic acid, which forms in wine made by a faulty technique, for example if fermentation takes place at too high a temperature or excess exposure to the air causes a bacterial infection.

The other side of the dry/sweet scale is accounted for by sugar. Now there's plenty of sugar in grapes, of course, but what counts here is 'residual' sugar – the sweetness left in the wine after fermentation and blending. There will always be a little residual sugar in a wine, even one which has been completely fermented out (in which, in other words, yeasts have converted all the grape sugar into alcohol). Most so-called dry wines contain between 1 and 5 grams per litre (g/l) sugar, but this can vary wildly. In Germany, their dry *trocken* wines can contain up to 9g/l sugar. In terms of taste, there is a vital link between sugar and acidity because the two balance each other. German producers are practised in gauging their level of sugar in the finished wine according to its acidity.

Another key element is tannin. There are grape skin tannins, grape pip tannins, stalk tannins and tannins from grape juice itself. All these tannins differ according to grape varieties and even according to the type of wood in casks used for ageing wines. Also, the nature of the tannins is significantly altered by the growing conditions.

However, you can take it as a general rule that wines containing large quantities of tannins will taste drier than those with less. Tannins have a drying effect because of their ability to bind with the protein receptors of the tongue. Chew a grape pip if you want to demonstrate this to yourself. What makes most red wines taste dry is a combination of low residual sugar and high tannin. White wines contain much less tannin than reds, although barrel-aged whites will pick up some tannin from the wood.

Fruit ripeness is the other big factor. The process of ripening on the vine has a profound and complex effect on the chemical constituents of the grape. In general terms, the riper the grape, the lower the acidity and the higher the natural sugar available for fermentation into alcohol. In marginal cool-climate regions such as Burgundy, the grapes often simply don't get ripe enough for the sugar to reach the necessary potential alcohol level for making balanced wine. So in poorer vintages, winemakers have to chaptalize (add sugar to) the grape must before fermentation.

Wines made with added sugar (and we're talking cane sugar of the type you'd put on your porridge) will lack the fullness and generosity of those from better vintages. They'll tend towards higher acidity and harsher, unripe tannins – factors that make the wines taste drier and leaner. Hot countries don't have this problem. If anything, producers in Languedoc or Chile, Australia or South Africa may have to strive to make wines that are not too soft or sweet to the taste.

DID THE BRITISH INVENT CHAMPAGNE!?

Britons drink more champagne than anyone except the French. Why do we love it so much? Possibly because we invented it! The French dispute this, of course, but it has long been known that British wine merchants created the first man-made sparkling wine through a discovery they made about the still wines they were importing from the Champagne region in the seventeenth century.

The wines were delicate and valuable, and were shipped in bottles because they would not stay fresh in cask. The cold climate of the region meant that the wines were often not fully fermented out by the time they were bottled. In the warm of the following spring, the yeasts would reawaken to feed on the grape sugar still remaining. The gas produced from this new fermentation could not escape from the sealed bottle and thus made it slightly fizzy.

Being clever chaps, the Brits soon worked out the biochemistry, figuring out ways to increase the sugar levels, and make the twice-fermented wine even more fizzy. They produced specially strengthened, reusable bottles for the purpose, and successfully experimented with methods of boosting the second fermentation.

There is documentary evidence of this, because an Englishman, Christopher Merret, presented a paper to the Royal Society in 1662 describing how it was all done. The effect, Merret explained, was to induce a second fermentation, which, taking place in a closed bottle, causes the resulting carbon dioxide to integrate with the wine as bubbles.

This was all before Dom Pérignon arrived at the Abbey of Hautvillers near the region's winemaking capital, Epernay, in 1668, where he has been mistakenly credited with 'inventing' champagne in the ancient cellars many years later.

Just like port and sherry, champagne is an adaptation of a far less interesting basic product. All these great wines owe their very existence to the enterprising wine merchants of Britain, who created them abroad for the pleasure of drinkers back home and thus created the respective major industries that now thrive in Portugal, Spain and France.

SALTY TALE: MANZANILLA

Manzanilla is the sherry the Spanish drink. Served icy cold, it is the pale, dry and tangy fortified wine of Sanlucar de Barrameda, an outpost of the sherry region on the Atlantic seaside. But while manzanilla is the national aperitif all over Spain, it is scarcely known further afield. The dry sherry preferred in the wider world is fino, made famous by brands such as Tio Pepe and La Ina, and produced in the sherry capital, Jerez.

In Jerez – the word 'sherry' is simply an anglicization of the town's name – they like to tell you fino is their own invention, but it isn't. The Jerezanos got the idea from their seaside counterparts in Sanlucar. I went to the fountainhead to hear the story first hand, from leading manzanilla producer Hidalgo, which has the bodega for its La Gitana brand in the town centre, just 500 metres from the Atlantic ocean.

'The humidity and temperature here are absolutely essential to the creation of the wine. The conditions are unique to the location so close to the sea, and it is often said that manzanilla has a salty tang to it thanks to the ocean breezes,' Tim Holt, then the export manager, told me as we padded along the compacted earth floor between dark canyons of sherry butts stacked four high into the *criaderas* – 'nurseries' of maturing sherry – that have slumbered in this vast, cathedral-like building for more than a century.

It is in these thousands of oak casks, some of them even older than Hidalgo itself (the business was founded in 1792) that the basic dry white wine of the region, mildly fortified with spirit to a strength of 15 per cent alcohol, undergoes its miraculous transformation into manzanilla.

On this very hot day we had already been to the vineyards on the gentle slopes just a short drive inland, where Hidalgo grows the palomino grapes for the wines on their estate at Il Cuadrado. The vines are low to the ground, their fruit ripe to bursting under the baking sun, and roasted all the more by the ultraviolet light reflected back from the chalky white soil known here as *albariza* – the most valued of all terrains in the sherry region.

So engorged are the grapes they need just a moderate crushing, rather than pressing, to give up all the juice needed for the year's new wine. This use only of the 'free-run' juice ensures that the basic product is a very high-quality one – what the French would grandly call a *première cuvée*.

The juice is fermented at the large, hi-tech winery at Il Cuadrado and then fortified with colourless, neutral spirit to stabilize the delicate white wine and help preserve its freshness. Later, the new wine is delivered to the bodega to begin the long process of conversion into sherry.

Hidalgo makes all kinds of sherry including the pale, dry fino associated with Jerez. However, the method of making manzanilla is original to Sanlucar. It is a very odd process, devised in the town in the early 1800s. Until this time, all sherry was oxidized and thus brown in colour, because it was inevitably exposed to the air inside the casks as it matured. But then, someone in Sanlucar came across a means of keeping the maturing wine pale and fresh for years on end. It had long been noticed that when new wine was run into the maturing casks, a layer of fluffy white scum would form on top of the liquid. It was composed of yeast cells, nourished by the nutrients in the wine, and stimulated to further growth by the wild yeasts present in the air of the bodegas. Naturally, the winemakers tended to skim this unattractive film off the wine, thinking it harmful.

The opposite, however, turned out to be the case. In an inspired experiment, a cask was left with the frothy coating intact, and the sherry did not oxidize, but stayed a white-wine colour. What's more, it took on a pungent, tangy flavour with a freshness and zest probably unknown at the time. Before long, winemakers such as Don Eduardo Hidalgo, ancestor of the present owners, were devising means of producing pale, dry sherries in this style on a commercial scale. They started to call the frothy crust on the wine the *flor* – flower, as it resembled a bloom – and worked out how to keep it alive, by continuously 'refreshing' the casks with new, nutrient-bearing wine. In the local metaphor, 'the young wine is taught by the older wine'.

Today, this continuous process is embodied in the *criadera* system of a series of casks, perhaps hundreds of them, through which new wines of five, six or more succeeding vintages are progressively blended on the way to the final series of casks, known as the *solera* – meaning simply 'soil' – because they are at the last stage of the process before the wine is run off for filtering and bottling, on ground level.

It's a strange but picturesque process, and the resulting wine is as much a thrilling revelation today as it must have been to those pioneers of two centuries ago.

Manzanilla – the name probably comes from that of a nearby winemaking village once known for its pale, dry table wines – remains unique. Because Sanlucar is by the sea, the air in its bodegas is uniquely stable, making it possible to maintain the ideal temperatures and consistent high humidity that foster the growth of the *flor*.

Sanlucar winemakers assert that the pale, dry fino sherry of Jerez is a mere imitation of manzanilla, and reckon it was about 50 years before the Jerezanos managed to copy the style successfully. Today, some fino bodegas in Jerez have elaborate pipework systems installed high above the *criaderas* to spray fine water mists into the air. The aim is to maintain the sort of humidity that comes naturally in Sanlucar, but the unique nature of manzanilla is forever beyond replication.

JUST A DETAIL ABOUT ORIGINS

In most European nations, regulations insist that the names of wines correspond strictly with their place of origin. If the label says Chablis, the wine must come entirely from within that Burgundian region's boundaries. If it says Chianti Classico, it must originate in a legally defined zone of Tuscany's Chianti hills. And so on.

In California, where until recently they made wines of all sorts, cheerfully labelling them with names like Chablis and Chianti, the rules are still being tightened up. In 2006, the state's governor, Arnold Schwarzenegger, signed a new law for the County of Sonoma. Wines labelled Sonoma should come from grapes grown within the county, he decreed, because 'Sonoma is a premier appellation known around the world of which consumers expect that the wine actually comes from Sonoma.'

But Schwarzenegger has cut the county's growers a bit of slack. Not all the wine under their labels needs to be from Sonoma – just 75 per cent of it.

THE THREE CUPS OF WINE PHILOSOPHY

Why are bottles the size they are for everything from champagne to port as well as 'table' wines – at the universal 75 centilitres? It is a little more than $1\frac{1}{3}$ pints, which doesn't tell us much. The precise quantity of 75cl dates only from 1979, when weights and measures legislation in the US and the European Economic Community simultaneously (and probably collaboratively) decreed the size. Previously, capacity had ranged more or less from 68cl to 76cl. But why this sort of size at all? Why not a pint, or a litre? It's a proper mystery, and if there is a solution, it probably lies with the ancient Greeks. In their philosophy, three cups of wine was the prescribed dose for civilized drinkers. The first was for health, the second for pleasure, the third for sleep. Subsequent pourings would bring, in turn, only inebriation, sickness, violence, madness.

Today's bottle size, as it happens, provides six 125ml glassfuls, or three apiece for two people. This glass size also approximates to a modern 'unit' of alcohol. Is it coincidence that we are recommended for our health to drink no more than two or three such units per day?

And then there is the question of why wine comes in dozens. Why not in metric tens? France, after all, is the modern home of metrication as well as the world's leading wine nation. But it turns out that it is Britain, the world's leading wine importer, that set the number.

Until the seventeenth century, wines of all kinds were shipped and sold in casks. Glass bottles were expensive to produce, delicate, bulbous and difficult to seal. They were not used to keep wine in for any length of time; they acted only as decanters in homes, and doubled as measures in inns and taverns. But in the 1650s, an inventive West Country gent, Sir Kenelm Digby, devised a means of producing a sturdy glass bottle with a reinforcing punt in its base. It was simply an experiment, but an adapted version was soon in use by wine merchants in Bristol and London to bottle champagne. Before long, consignments of this 'English bottle' were being sent over to the Champagne region, so the winemakers there could bottle sparkling wine for their British customers *in situ*.

It was from Digby's prototype that the first mass-produced glass bottles derived. The capacity of the original was probably about 1¼ pints. Perhaps Sir Kenelm's classical education made him aware of ancient Greek axiom, as aforementioned, or more likely the size simply came out this way in the blowing process. It certainly turned out to be convenient, because the usual wine-shipping cask, a hogshead, held about 50 gallons. This could be decanted into a neat number of English bottles: 25 dozen.

By 1800 and the onset of the Industrial Revolution, the cylindrical, relatively narrow, long-necked and flat-bottomed bottles of the kind we know today were in large-scale production. In the 1790s, producers and merchants in Britain and all over Europe had discovered they could stopper these bottles with long corks driven into the necks. Wines could now be packed into crates and sold ready-bottled. And they were – by the dozen.

Progressive metrication from the nineteenth century onwards has made no impression at the retail end of the worldwide wine industry. But maybe change is on the way. In 2005, Helm Wines of Murrumbateman, New South Wales, was nominated for an Australian Capital Territory Occupational Health and Safety Award for its introduction of 'decimal dozen' wine cases of ten bottles. More than half of wine purchases in Australia are made by women, and the state's Occupational Health and Safety legislation forbids female lifting of weights above 15 kilograms. Some cases of wine weigh as much as 20 kilograms. Helm makes highly rated Riesling wines and other varietals, all of them sold by the ten-bottle case.

WINES AND ALCOHOL CONTENT

I have a friend who applies certain fixed criteria to his choice of wines. One of these concerns alcoholic strength. He won't touch anything under 13 per cent, and if he finds anything at 14 per cent or above, he is prepared to be flexible about another treasured criterion, price.

Strong wine and good wine are not synonymous, but weak wine and bad wine are. Not that this makes alcohol levels a reliable guide to good and bad wines. No one would sensibly claim, for example, that a great Mosel Spätlese at 7 or 8 per cent is in any way inferior to a grand Sauternes at 14 or 15 per cent. The difference is in style, not quality.

But why are some wines so much more alcoholic than others?

In the natural order of things, the big factor is, as anyone remotely acquainted with the wonders of photosynthesis would know, the weather. Sunshine and temperature are the principal ingredients when it comes to ripening grapes, and thus raising the sugar content level to a point that makes them fit for turning into wine.

Typically, ripened grapes are composed between 15 and 25 per cent of sugar. In the lingo, the 'must weight' – the proportion of sugar in the new-pressed juice prior to fermentation – is the measure of the ripeness of the grapes, and thus of the potential alcohol content of the wine. Come harvest time, it is the must weight, gauged according to a scale, that determines when the grapes are ideal for picking.

The two scales familiar in Europe are Oechsle in Germany and Baumé in France (and elsewhere). Both systems are related to the specific gravity scale, with Oechsle simply an expression of it. Baumé can be more directly seen to relate to alcohol levels, being worked out on the basis that, during fermentation, about half the grape sugar will be lost as carbon dioxide and the rest will turn into alcohol. Thus, must composed 24 per cent of sugar will rate around 12 degrees on the Baumé scale, and produce wine of about 12 degrees alcohol.

These figures are not exact Baumé measurements, and there are plenty of variables, such as the types of yeasts involved in the fermentation, which can materially affect alcohol levels. But the major variant is human interference. In the north – let us say most of Europe – the weather is not to be relied upon. Every season has the potential to deliver too little of the sunshine necessary to push those ripening grapes high enough up the Oechsle and Baumé scales to reach the potential alcohol required by the producer, or demanded under the innumerable standards set by the European Union or other national wine-quality regulators.

So what does a wine producer do when autumn's chill arrives before the grapes have begun to register the prayed-for measurement on the scale? Two choices: pray harder, or chaptalize. The latter option, in nomenclature not without its own whiff of orison, is named after one Jean-Antoine Chaptal. He was not a churchman, however, but the agriculture minister in the government of Napoleon Bonaparte in 1800, who sponsored (maybe even devised) this process of 'improving' wine. It's simple enough. The method is to add sugar to the must during fermentation to raise the weight to the level at which it will produce the desired alcohol level.

One of the greater surprises in store for casual visitors to wineries in Europe is to find sacks of refined sugar stacked on the premises. And given that it takes up to 20g of sugar to add one degree of alcohol to a litre of must, you're looking at sugar in bulk: up to 400 kilos to raise the contents of a 10,000-litre vat by a couple of degrees.

Of course it's all rigorously controlled. Throughout wine-producing Europe, EU directives or local regulations specify that must weights have to reach certain minimum levels before chaptalization will be allowed. The levels vary according to the northerliness of the vineyards. There are limits on the amount of sugar that can be added, and on the maximum alcohol content of the finished wine. This rather shuts the door on the production of high-alcohol wines in all but the warmest regions.

The upshot is that in northernmost Europe table wines (including champagne) 12 degrees is the upper end of the norm. Only as you move south will the prevailing weather, and regulations, permit the stronger stuff. In Bordeaux, occasional years will yield red wines above 12.5 per cent, which is scarcely a worry to the growers there, as high alcohol is by no means their objective. But travel further south, and it's a different story.

Châteauneuf du Pape, in the deep south of the Rhône Valley, is a good example. The AC rules here insist that the wine must reach a minimum of 12.5 per cent, but the growers are quite used to their *cuvées* producing 13.5, even 14.5. No need for chaptalization here, and the process is outlawed in many of Europe's warmest regions anyway.

In the south, and in particular in the southern hemisphere, the problem with grape must reverses. There can be too much sugar, and not enough of the natural acidity needed to give the vital balance of flavour in the finished wine. And, yes, the answer is indeed to interfere with nature, and to add acid during the fermentation.

So the seeker after high-strength wines should look to the south. Australian and New Zealand Chardonnays start at about 13, and Antipodean reds are quite ordinarily 14 or higher. There are plenty of quality wines of strength to be found in Argentina and Chile, too, and Spain and Portugal have growing numbers of new (or newly marketed) wines from emerging regions such as Somontano and Alentejo at high strengths. Italy has had a name for strong wines for longer. Barolo and Barbaresco never lack muscle and there are hefties too among Tuscan denominations such as Montalcino. Verona's monster Recioto wines are worth seeking out.

Sweet wines, made from grapes that are late-picked and achieve the most extraordinary Baumé levels, are a law unto themselves. Sauternes are commonly 14 or 15 per cent, but less-valued stickies from the likes of Monbazillac can be just as powerful (I have heard of Monbazillacs in recent vintages being sold at 17 per cent) and are considerably cheaper.

These are all table wines, of course. Fortified wines in the port, madeira and sherry mould are quite different, acquiring their extra strength through the addition of spirit either during or after fermentation. Pale, dry sherries, however, carry less of a clout than they used to. They are typically a mere 15 per cent alcohol, thanks to modern winemaking and punitive excise, but none the worse for it. Ports at 20 per cent plus are actually higher in alcohol than their ancestors, but are now of a quality undreamed of in the early days, when the three-bottle men could have their quota by noon and still stand up.

WHICH NATION DRINKS THE MOST?

Welcome, then, to the transforming world of wine. And the changes are not all at the production end. The pattern of worldwide consumption has lately altered beyond recognition. Back in 1970, the deepest drinkers of wine were the French. They were getting through 153 bottles a year for every man, woman and child in the population. The Italians were just a bottle or two behind. In 2007, France was at number two (behind, weirdly, Luxembourg) at 73 bottles a year. Italy was still next, but down to 65 bottles a year. In both countries, consumption had more than halved (while in Luxembourg it had nearly doubled from 40 to 76 bottles).

Although the United States is a leading producer of wine, in states including Oregon, New York and Washington as well as California, its own people have proved reluctant consumers. Even as the Californian wine industry exploited the wine boom in export markets such as Britain between 1970 and 1990, annual consumption per head in the US inched only modestly from six bottles to ten bottles per annum over the period. Between 1990 and 2008, Americans kept up the pace, and currently get through 16 bottles a year.

These changes at the top of the league represent the end of a

long chapter of habitual wine drinking. In wine-producing countries for much of the nineteenth and twentieth centuries, it was
routine for working people to drink a bottle or two every day, just
as it was once the norm for their counterparts in Britain to drink
a gallon of ale with the same dedicated regularity. In spite of the
hysteria over 'binge-drinking' today, the relative excesses of the all-
too-recent past are now firmly consigned to history. High prices,
punitive taxation, official disapproval and the growing obsession
with health will forever position wine as an indulgence luxury to be
enjoyed only in moderation.

This, no doubt, is a very good thing. But it does put a limit on
the market. Wine is always going to be a luxury; it will never regain
its place in the staple diet, even of wine-producing nations. Britain,
amazingly enough, is the biggest importer of wine in the world, and
yet annual per capita consumption is a mere 25 bottles a year. This
is a magnificent improvement on the four bottles being drunk back
in 1970, but the trend towards wine – which has contributed to the
halving of beer consumption – is already flattening out. Industry
forecasters do not expect British drinkers to get through significantly more wine in the future than they do already. And while new
customers might well be found in the boom economies of Asia, it
might be some time before Western habits such as a glass of claret
with the Sunday roast catch on with anyone other than the well-
travelled wealthy.

OPENINGS AND CLOSURES

Wine has its nerdy side. Those who make and sell it get very exer-
cised, for example, about boring trivia such as corks. Some members

of the trade have complained that one in ten corks is so bad it spoils the wine. This is manifestly ridiculous, but there's enough talk to have generated lots of business for manufacturers of beastly plastic substitutes, and more recently, screw caps.

The fuss has been great enough even for the drinking public to start taking notice. Some of us, reportedly, go red in the face not with the effort of extracting recalcitrant corks, but at the very notion of substituting the real thing with the sort of 'closure' previously only found on whisky bottles. The ritual of drawing the cork, they splutter, accounts for a fair measure of the enjoyment to be had from a bottle of wine.

On the other hand, numerous wine producers, particularly outside Europe, have dropped natural corks altogether because of the alleged plague of taint, and are now being joined by powerful retailers who insist that their wine suppliers adopt screw caps if they wish to continue doing business. It's all slightly sinister, because the traditional cork producers, who harvest their raw material from sustainable oak forests in some of Europe's most beautiful and wildlife-rich regions, are trying very hard to put things to rights, and surely could do with some moral and material support.

As to other practical matters, the questions of getting the cork out, letting wine breathe and whether to 'lay it down' or drink it straight away continue to cause mild dismay. I hope the following might provide moderate enlightenment.

TWISTS AND TURNS

On the morning I set out for the cork forests of Portugal in the summer of 2003, an announcement arrived in the post from a top

New Zealand wine company. It was headlined: VILLA MARIA SAYS SCREW CORKS.

Villa Maria's owner, George Fistonich, was nailing his colours to the vine post. He would sell no more wine in bottles with corks. 'We are 100 per cent committed to the quality that the use of screw-cap closures guarantees,' he declared. 'To achieve this, Villa Maria has had to inform distributors that it is screw caps or nothing. This may seem a little harsh, but no other industry in the world accepts the type of product failure experienced using cork.'

Reading this at the airport, waiting for the plane to Lisbon, I began to wonder if Mr Fistonich might be objecting just a little too much. True, we have all heard of 'corked' wine, but after centuries of happily confining wine in bottles with nothing else, is the cork really dead?

There are plenty of winemakers, and retailers, who think so. One in five bottles now has either a plastic stopper or a screw cap. It's due to a recent surge in the number of wines spoiled by a taint known as 2,4,6 trichloroanisole, or TCA, which imparts an unpleasant, musty aroma and flavour – and has been blamed roundly on the cork manufacturers.

And so to Portugal, where the country's – and the world's – biggest cork producer, Amorim, had invited me to see for myself what is being done about it. I was met by Carlos de Jesus, Amorim's marketing director, who conducted me to the cork oak forests, starting an hour's drive north-east of Lisbon and extending over hundreds of square miles beyond. It was the harvest, and men armed with light, broad-bladed axes were stripping the trunks and lower branches of the trees of their bark, up to three inches thick, in sections several feet long. The process takes place once every nine years.

'It's like a face peel in beauty treatment,' Carlos told me. 'It leaves the skin a little tender, but renewed. We harvest between May and August, when growth is at its most active. The first harvest is after 25 years. It does the trees no harm. They live up to 200 years.'

This is obviously the most natural and renewable means of providing the raw material for bottle stoppers. And I do wonder how the wine industry could ever have adopted cork-shaped stoppers made from what Carlos likes to call 'oil-derived products' instead.

But plastic 'corks' look doomed. They can be difficult to extract and hard to unwind from the corkscrew afterwards. It's impossible to push them back into the bottle. They utterly lack the indispensable elasticity of natural cork. It is the screw cap that is the only real long-term rival for cork. It obviates the corkscrew, and may, in time, prove to be as good at preserving the wine in healthy condition, as well as being proof against tainted flavour.

Back in the forest, we next visited a huge Amorim plant where the peeled bark is stacked in endless canyons, several metres high, before being boiled in newly installed vats incorporating a continuous water-filtering system to remove impurities and combat the dreaded taint. 'In the last two and a half years we have spent 43 million dollars on re-equipping to fight TCA,' Carlos explained. It's a candid admission that the infection has indeed been a problem for this major industry, which employs 20,000 people in Portugal.

Extensive research suggests that the taint has become more common due to chemical reactions with chlorine products used in the wine industry. But Carlos was quick to point out that TCA does not affect only cork. 'It can adhere to wood, to concrete, to metal and to plastic – including oil-derived stoppers and screw caps too,' he said, adding that a major winery in the USA had lately traced the TCA in its wine to an infection not in its corks but in its drainage system. The infection was so severe the entire plant had to be closed down.

The task at Amorim is to ensure that all the three billion corks they produce annually are TCA free. And they are succeeding. It's down to changed practices in the company's dozen production centres, including a new steam-treatment system, specifically developed to counter TCA, through which every single cork passes. The company has also installed gas chromatography equipment to detect any infections.

I was greatly impressed with what Amorim has achieved and, as the world's biggest manufacturer, the company, founded in 1870, continues to do great things to restore the good name of its own corks, if not the many more that are made by other producers in Portugal, Spain and around the world. In 2008 Amorim launched an entertaining online campaign called 'Save Miguel'. Miguel turned out to be a young cork oak, and did much to highlight the eco factor, for example, that screwcaps generate 24 times more CO_2 than corks.

But can Amorim hope to impress winemakers such as George Fistonich? Since 2003, Fistonich has been joined by most of the other New Zealand producers in rejecting natural corks and substituting them with screw caps.

Company chairman Antonio Amorim acknowledges that views have become polarized. 'In Europe cork and wine is an old marriage. It's accepted,' he told me. 'But in the New World they question everything and I don't blame them for that.' He concedes that his own industry was slow to respond to the TCA crisis back in the

1990s, as the wine trade started to blame every duff bottle on TCA-affected corks, even though cork was really only responsible for a fraction of the total.

'Ten years ago in this industry we could only talk philosophy, but now we can talk science,' he said. 'TCA is a problem we feel we have solved, although I would never claim to have eradicated it. But now we can start to speak about the many positive aspects of cork, how it contributes to the good of wine, to its health and development.'

He seems calmly confident, and is prepared for a long campaign of championing the cork. 'We are patient people,' he says. 'After all we wait 25 years to collect our first harvest, and we are prepared to take time to convince consumers that this natural product is the best one for now and for the future.'

CORKSCREWS – LOSING THE THREAD

My waiter's friend finally gave up the ghost one Christmas, at least 20 years after it was given to me in a party bag at a Bordeaux tasting hosted by the Union des Grands Crus Classés. The Union's name was boldly emblazoned on the implement, so I assume the gift was intended as an aid to promotion. It certainly worked, in more senses than one. Resembling an oversized clasp knife with foldable lever and 'worm', it was easily the best corkscrew I have ever had.

This type of device, so known because it is portable and can be used to extract corks with dignified economy of effort under the beady eyes of restaurant customers, was first made in 1883, by a German engineer called Karl Wienke. I didn't know it was a German invention until later, but I was not surprised to find out when I did. Naturally, once the screw had snapped off my vintage model, I went out in urgent search of an identical replacement.

The first purchase, which looked much the same, bent beyond redemption after only a couple of extractions. The second, more substantial and twice the price, had a sort of claw designed to fit over the bottle's mouth, presumably to give better purchase under the pressure exerted on the lever as the cork is withdrawn. But the claw tore into the flank of the cork as it was extracted, and tended to chip the glass where it ground into the rim. This is not ideal. This instrument must have been designed by an imbecile. I threw it away and have since acquired a better, safer model with an ingenious hinged lever that lets you pull out the cork in two distinct movements.

Before acquiring this, however, I did try out a few alternatives along the way. I tried all the simple pull corkscrews that had been lurking forever in the back of the kitchen drawer. They worked fine, but in some cases, especially with plastic 'corks', made the task possible only with eye-bulging, knee-trembling effort. Bad idea.

I did have a Screwpull for a while. This clever notion, the invention of Texas oil engineer Herbert Allen, is apparently a miniature version of a drilling rig. The principle of the continuous turn, which threads the worm through the cork and extracts it from the bottle, is indeed ingenious. The worm is Teflon coated, which allegedly makes the process of driving the screw into the cork about five times easier than otherwise. My Screwpull, unhappily, had a short life. The non-stick coating wore away and it became very difficult to drive the worm in. If this is still a problem with more recent models, it would make me hesitate before buying another, as they are not cheap. As for the 'ultimate' Screwpull, an ergonomic device that looks as if it might be an instrument of medieval torture but does extract corks with an effortless single lever action, I recommend it for anyone with the money and a big enough kitchen drawer, mostly because it not only yanks the cork out, but unwinds it from the worm afterwards. This is a major plus, because the polymer (plastic) bungs now commonly used to substitute for the real thing can be such a swine to remove from the screw. It is to be hoped these horrible products will before long be rendered obsolete by screw caps, but in the meantime any device that expedites their removal, so to speak, gets my blessing.

I do appeal to manufacturers not to produce any more of the old-fashioned, but depressingly persistent twin-lever metal corkscrews. These are the elaborate, usually chrome-finished contraptions with wing-like levers which rise on a ratchet as the worm is driven in. The wings are then manhandled downwards to extract the cork. I have never found one that worked satisfactorily.

Given the great variety of shapes, lengths and materials employed for closing bottles nowadays, corkscrew manufacturers need to develop instruments which will cope with the greatest number of eventualities. Far too many corks break up as soon as pierced because the worm has a blunt point and is so bulky it cannot be accurately centred. Long corks in grand old wines are a particular problem. They need a corkscrew with a long worm which will penetrate the whole length of the cork. If the thread reaches only halfway through, it will very likely leave the lower half of the cork behind in the neck. These residues are then hellish difficult to extract without scattering quantities of dusty residue into the nectar beneath. Also extremely difficult to remedy is the problem of a cork that won't grip the worm, ploughing up its centre and leaving a mushy core.

It's probably a good idea to have to hand a butler's thief or twist-and-wiggle cork remover in case of such emergencies. These are the pronged utensils that slide a steel strip down each side of the cork and grip it as the pulling force is exerted. The thief in the name perpetuates the myth that butlers could open bottles with these implements without leaving tell-tale signs of penetration after swigging some of the wine and then shoving the cork back in. This is a miserable libel on the good name of butlers.

COUPE DE GLASS

It is a popular misconception that champagne was originally drunk from glasses with saucerlike bowls of a shape inspired by the profile of Marie-Antoinette's bosom. Champagne was being served in flute glasses (with slim conical bowls) long before this Queen of France was born in 1755. The *coupe* was popularized only in the twentieth century, but fizzled out almost as fast as its inappropriate shape took the sparkle out of the wine.

Marie-Antoinette, who was Austrian and not French, has been the victim of every kind of republican black propaganda since the Revolution that broke out in 1789 and to which she lost her life in 1793. The connection drawn between her person and the *coupe* is no more than a retelling of myths concerning both Madame du Barry and Madame de Pompadour, royal mistresses of a previous generation.

The breast-shaped wine-glass tradition has been said to originate in Greek mythology. A drinking vessel, the story goes, was modelled for Paris, Prince of Troy, on the bosom of Helen, the most beautiful woman in the world, whom he stole away from Menelaus, King

of Sparta, triggering the Trojan War. The glass in question is known even today as the Paris goblet.

Those who swallow this sort of nonsense might also be willing to believe the report that the fashion designer for Chanel, Karl Lagerfeld, has designed a champagne glass especially for Dom Pérignon, inspired by the shape of the bosom of his compatriot, the model Claudia Schiffer. A further rumour has it that this item is available for sale at a price of $3,150, including a bottle of Dom Pérignon.

BORDEAUX AS STANDARD

Today's standard cylindrical, high-shouldered wine bottle is known as the 'Bordeaux' shape because its use was standardized first in the French wine region, from the 1790s. The cylinder shape allowed bottles to be stacked on their sides, allowing for the bottle-ageing of wine as distinct from cask-ageing. The first patent for moulded uniform bottles was held from 1821 by British manufacturer Rickettes, but mechanized mass production did not begin in France, at the factory of glass-maker Claude Boucher in Cognac, until 1894. For Bordeaux wines, regulators imposed a standard bottle size of 75cl in 1930, but this was widely ignored until enforcement by the EEC directive of 1979. Once a standard weight of 725 grams, the bottles are now very much lighter. Four principal standard weights are Traditional at 550 grams, Semi-Heavy at 460 grams, Standard at 400 grams and Light at 380 grams. Heavier, costlier bottles are usually reserved for wines intended for long keeping. The bottles are manufactured with a punt in the base, around which sediment collects, facilitating decanting. Lighter bottles are used for wines made for immediate consumption.

ORGANIC WINES

In anything other than the most ideal climate, it can be terribly hard to keep vines healthy without spraying against insects and diseases. While it's a reasonable assumption that grape growers minimize their use of expensive chemicals to save money, there are occasional alarms that residues from all those sprays get into the wine. In 2008, a campaign group called Pesticides Action Network Europe (PANE) published the results of analyses made of 40 bottles of wine from the Continent and the New World. Only the organic bottles, five out of the six tested, were found to be free of chemical taint. Twenty-four separate pesticides were identified, including five defined by the EU as carcinogenic or harmful to the human reproductive system. Among the contaminated wines were bottles from classified vineyards in Bordeaux and Burgundy priced at up to 200 euros.

'The presence of pesticides in European wines is a growing problem,' Elliott Cannell of PANE told the BBC. 'Many grape farmers are abandoning traditional methods of pest control in favour of using hazardous synthetic pesticides even though there is the risk of residues of classified toxins such as neutrigens and endocrinal disruptors.'

It all sounds scary enough, even if Mr Cannell admitted, as he did, that none of the bottles of wine tested presented an immediate hazard to health, at least from agrichemical residues. But news items like this must be music to those who make their wine by organic means, because while few would doubt the sincerity of the movement overall, there is scant evidence that organic foods and drinks are either more delicious or better for us than their mainstream counterparts.

The meaning of 'organic' is nowhere, yet, defined by law. In 2009, the European Union introduced proposed new legislation setting out terms of reference which would allow food and drink producers to display an official EU organic logo provided at least 95 per cent of the finished product could be appropriately certified. But besides an absolute interdict against genetically modified organisms, the terms of reference have yet to be defined. This regulation could be a long time in ratification.

Unofficial regulating bodies such as the UK's Soil Association and the California Certified Organic Farmers don't use the term 'organic wine' without at least qualifying it as shorthand for 'wine made from organically grown grapes'. The problem is that while it's possible to forswear chemicals in the vineyard, the same cannot be done in the winery. It is near impossible (though not unknown) to make drinkable wine without the use of sulphur products. These control the bacteria that would otherwise turn the wine into vinegar, or worse. Under prevailing regulations in both the EU and the US, all wine, organic or not, made with the aid of sulphur products must carry the warning 'Contains sulphites'. Some people can suffer adverse reactions to sulphur, so it's fair enough.

I cannot say that I have detected any identifiable distinction between organic and non-organic wines, in spite of eagerly tasting hundreds of qualifying samples. And while plenty of well-known and admired wines are indeed organic, it remains true that few of the most revered and expensive wines in the world claim to be made in this way. On the other hand, organic wines no longer seem to carry any significant price premium. This is not true of most organic foods.

If You Ask My Advice

Can wine merchants be trusted to give good advice? Some. Berry Bros. & Rudd, in my own happy experience, is among them. The firm is often called 'the Queen's wine merchant' because it has a royal warrant from Her Majesty and has its shop just across the road from St James's Palace in London. Buck House is just round the corner in the big park. But this is not why I have such a soft spot for Berrys.

I have been an occasional customer for ever, and once took my two children, when they were quite little, to visit the shop. I thought they might be thrilled by the antiquated interior, which looks like something out of a Hogarth cartoon, and features a weighing machine from the days when Berrys was a general grocer. This contraption was retained when Berrys became a full-time wine merchant centuries ago, because their customers liked to be weighed on it. The firm has nine volumes from 1765 recording the avoirdupois of the good, the bad and the odious. Included are Beau Brummell and Lord Byron, William Pitt and Charles James Fox, Napoleon III and very much later, famous figures such as Lawrence Olivier and Vivien Leigh, not to mention more contemporary celebrities.

None of this much impressed my young children. On the contrary, they were both rather spooked by the old shop, with its steeply sloping floors, dark corners and grave-looking pinstriped assistants. I was disappointed they did not share my enthusiasm for what to me was, and remains, my favourite of all London emporiums.

But time goes by. Both the children grew up and escaped our sequestered Somerset life by enrolling at London universities. And then one Christmas they presented me with a bottle of wine in a very smart Berry Bros. box. They had saved up, travelled all the way from Bloomsbury to the shop (a miracle of navigation, I'd say) and told the assistant they had this much to spend and wanted the best bottle of claret available for the money, for their dad.

Now how many wine merchants would you trust to play it straight when presented with a pair of punters like this? Wide-eyed undergraduates without much to spend might well be expected to be treated, in such a very regal old merchant's, with condescension at best. But that's not the way, according to the children's reports, that it went at all. There was a brief discussion as to whether the wine was desired for keeping or for drinking fairly soon, and then a bottle of Château Pichon-Lalande 1997 was produced. It was in budget, and came recommended. They didn't have a clue whether it was a good buy or not. But when I received it on Christmas Day, with delirious (all right, tearful) appreciation, I knew it was a very good buy indeed. The children had been treated with courtesy and were sold a great wine from an affordable (rather than overrated and price-bloated) vintage. They were given the same consideration as Byron or Vivien Leigh might have expected, except that, as far as I know, no one offered to weigh them.

I told the children what a wonderful, if extravagant, gift this was and what a good wine. They believed me, because some time later

I shared it with them. And they have since given me a few other wines from Berrys, each as well chosen, by all parties concerned, as the first. The children have entirely lost their fear of the shop, and even claim they enjoy making forays there. They are both now earning their livings in London, and I look forward to hearing one day that they might just pop in to buy a little something for themselves.

This is one of the things I believe makes the world of wine such a happy place to live in, and in which to bring up children.

UPS AND DOWNS

How wine prices change. At the retail end of the business, they go up, never down, but in relation to each other the variations can be dramatic. Consider these prices, all per standard bottle in the old money, with translations, from the list of Bristol merchant Harvey's for 1961–2. The figures to the right are the very approximate current cost of the equivalent wines from recent years of equivalent reputation.

Harvey's Bristol Cream sherry	25/6	(£1.27)	£8
Dow's Vintage Port 1947	25/9	(£1.28)	£60
Château Ausone 1953	17/3	(86p)	£1,000
Château Lafite 1953	36/3	(£1.31)	£800
Château D'Yquem 1948	30/9	(£1.54)	£150
Richebourg DRC 1955	49/9	(£2.48)	£1,000
JJ Prum Wehlener Sonnenuhr Riesling Auslese 1957	42/3	(£2.11)	£30
Moët & Chandon Brut	26/-	(£1.30)	£25
Chianti Ruffino (litre)	15/6	(77p)	£7

WHAT DO YOU DRINK WITH KETCHUP?

The conventions associated with wine are little more than obvious common sense. You know the sort of thing: drink white wine with fish; serve red wine at room temperature; never drink wine (except sherry) with soup. They were once enshrined in etiquette, but while they might have some gustatory significance, they have no place in the realm of social manners.

And yet, and yet. Relaxed though we might think we all are about wine – 'I don't know anything about it but I know what I like' – there are still anxieties. Food-and-wine matching is the main source of discomfort. It filters into the consciousness via the continuing custom in grand restaurants of employing sommeliers, previously known as wine waiters (the female of the species is a recent innovation), to counsel gastronomically aware diners on what goes with

what. It's also now common for restaurants to offer 'tasting menus' of endless miniature courses accompanied by glasses of wine, each suggested as the perfect 'partner'.

The principle seems to be that if you're going to pay a fortune for a glass or a bottle of wine, you might as well have one that goes with the food. This is all very well, but it does foster a culture of wine–food conformity. Customers start to believe that restaurants' suggestions are holy writ. This is regressive. Before we know it, we'll be back to white wine with fish.

The bolder kind of wine drinker pays no heed to advice, of course, and it is the budget that defines choice for most of us more than highfalutin advice ever will. We would all no doubt like to take Hugh Johnson up on some of the suggestions in his *Pocket Wine Book*, the biggest-selling wine book in the world: Chablis, Meursault or Corton-Charlemagne with a piece of cod; Vega Sicilia with well-hung game. But I suspect even Hugh's readers' primary concerns are more the other way round. You found a pretentious bottle of Aussie Shiraz at half price in the supermarket on the way back from work. Is there anything in the fridge you can drink it with? My advice is, if all you've got is fish fingers, give it a try. But go easy on the ketchup.

PASS THE PORT

Some wine conventions are more interesting than others. Passing the port to the left is an amusing diversion, but it has no mystique. It has always been the custom, simply because most of us are right-handed. At table, we know it is bad form to pass any item in front of a neighbour. By passing the port to the left, we always pass it in front of ourselves.

Socially astute guests won't care, but for those to whom this is one of the great issues of our time, the best advice is straightforward. Never accept an invitation to dinner from people whose reaction to the gift of a bottle of wine (or the absence of such a gift) is one that cannot comfortably be predicted. In practical terms, this might mean accepting no invitations from people who have not already dined at your house. That way, when receiving a reciprocal invitation, you need do no more than remember whether or not they brought wine with them in the first place.

There is no universal rule of etiquette to go by, because the casual drinking of wine is such a recent phenomenon. In the days when books of etiquette were written – they have, mercifully, long since died out – no one would have dreamed of taking bottles to anyone else's home. In the 1950s, when the practice seems to have started, there was a social injunction against taking wine to a host or hostess aged over 30, but this would now be a laughable form of discrimination.

Having decided whether or not to go equipped, the question of what kind of wine to take is a little bit trickier. Unless you have been asked by the host well in advance to contribute wine to the party, always assume your bottle will be treated as a gift, and that it is therefore unlikely to be opened on the night. This makes a true test of your generosity. In the unlikely event you know your host's taste, you should find a wine that conforms. If you wish to ingratiate yourself, be cautiously extravagant by choosing a bottle that is at least one step up from the basic. Avoid brands – the likes of Yellow Tail, Mouton Cadet or (God forbid) Blossom Hill – and seek out something from more recherché Australian producers such as Brown Bros., Peter Lehmann or De Bortoli. From Bordeaux, a *petit château* claret will do nicely, and from California anything but Blossom Hill, likewise.

'Dessert' wines – sweet whites from inexpensive French appellations such as Monbazillac, St Croix du Mont or Loupiac rather than madly expensive Barsac and Sauternes – can be fun, with the additional possibility that the host might open the bottle with pudding. Champagne is fine if you are ostensibly rich, but otherwise might backfire. You could be thought a show-off. If it has to be a sparkling wine, compromise with a *crémant* from Alsace, Burgundy or the Loire, a trendy Prosecco or one of the adventurous New World sparklers, such as California's Cuvée Napa.

Finally, if your hosts are vegetarians and you are to be treated to a flesh-free feast, remember you can take a suitable wine. Very many winemakers, and not merely 'organic' ones, now forswear the use of animal products (gelatine, isinglass and so on) for clarifying, and will proudly boast on their labels that the product is 'suitable for vegetarians'. In presenting the wine, proceed with caution. Remarks like 'Look, I've got you a veggie wine,' are superfluous. If your hosts are that sensitive they will examine the labels for themselves later and appreciate your thoughtfulness. This is preferable to the risk of giving them the impression you might be making light of their dietary preferences.

A UNIVERSAL OPINION

In his masterly guide to social survival, *Lifemanship*, BBC producer Stephen Potter touched on the topic of wine tasting. The novice drinker, asked for his opinion of a wine and having no clue whether it is good or bad, should venture, said Potter, that 'It is a little bit cornery.' This is sound advice.

SOME PRONUNCIATION

Wine names can be a minefield of mispronunciation for English speakers. We need to be warned, too, against *de trop* indigenous phonetics, and naff nicknames. With apologies to the sacred memory of Nancy Mitford and her *Noblesse Oblige* of 1956, there might have been a little addendum. U is OK; Non-U is inadvisable; Counter-U is unforgivable.

Bollinger *U*: Bollin-jer. *Non-U*: Bol-AN zhay. *Counter-U*: Bolly.

(Château) Cos-d'Estournel *U*: KOS destoornel. *Non-U*: KOH destoornel. *Counter-U*: Koz.

Gevrey-Chambertin *U*: Jevray SHAWM bertan. *Non-U*: Jevray SHAM bertin. *Counter-U*: Geoffrey Shambertan.

(Château) Lafite *U*: LAF eet. *Non-U*: La FEET. *Counter-U*: Laf EET Rothschild.

(Château) Lynch-Bages *U*: Linch Bahzh. *Non-U*: Lansch-Barge. *Counter-U*: Lunch Bags.

Moët *U*: M-wet. *Non-U*: Moh-ay. *Counter-U*: Moh-ay ette Shondon.

Montepulciano *U*: Montay pul chee AH no. *Non-U*: Montay pul see ANO. *Counter-U*: Monty pool chino.

Riesling *U*: REES-ling. *Non-U*: Ree-zling. *Counter-U*: RYE-zling.

Taittinger *U*: TAT in jer. *Non-U*: TAY tan jer. *Counter-U*: TAY tan zhay.

CHOOSING WINE IN
RESTAURANTS

Wine is centre stage in every kind of restaurant these days. Even in café-bar chains and pizzerias the length of the wine list might well outstretch that of the menu. The same goes for the prices. How to choose a wine you will like drinking and won't mind paying for? The first rule needs to be not to begrudge the cost. If you instinctively recoil from paying three times for a wine what you know it would cost you in a shop, drink something else, or stay at home.

The price you pay for wine in the better kind of restaurant is as much to do with the overall experience as it is with the wine itself. Margins on food are precarious, what with the fluctuating cost of the ingredients and the perpetually high cost of preparation and serving, not to mention the frightening overheads of the catering business. So it is quite usual for the wines to be marked up by 200 or 300 per cent.

That said, you have every right to expect a decent bottle. If you're eating in a chain restaurant, my advice is always to give the 'house' wine a try. Big chains take anything with their own name on it seriously, and have the kind of buying power that can obtain decent wines at reasonable cost.

And you don't have to buy wine by the bottle. Every kind of restaurant now offers wine by the glass. The dinky 125ml glass (one-sixth of a bottle) is now rare, so it is likely to be 175ml (a tad short of a quarter bottle) or the increasingly evident 250ml – a third of a bottle.

Ordering wine from a really grand list is something different. If you're new to wine, where do you start when you want something special but haven't a clue? At a place with a truly vast wine list, the Hotel du Vin in Bristol, Xavier Rousset urges customers just to ask. 'It's what we're here for,' says French-born Xavier, who is one of three sommeliers in the frantically busy bistro-style restaurant.

With a name like Hotel du Vin, the importance of wine to this fifteen-hotel chain is self-evident. The list is awesome – '. . . five to six hundred wines, some I haven't even tried myself,' says Xavier. 'When asked, we will suggest two or three different choices at different prices according to whether customers want a particular style of wine, or want advice on the right wine to match the dishes they have chosen.'

Xavier reckons that 'only about 5 per cent' of his customers really know a lot about wine, so no one need be afraid of admitting to ignorance. He has an important point here. If you are asking for help on choosing, do listen to what the sommelier says. You will get good advice if you're obviously open to it – interested rather than trying to show off your own knowledge.

As to self-help, Xavier recommends that if you have favourite wine producers, look on the list for anything with their name on it. 'For example, if you've had a Shiraz from d'Arenberg [a leading Australian outfit] and see one of their Cabernet Sauvignons, go for that – because it's the winemaker, rather than the region or country or even the grape variety, that is the main clue to a wine you'll like,' he says.

HOW LONG SHOULD YOU KEEP IT?

Scrutinizing the wine in a supermarket one day, I was rather impeded in my search for an Argentinian red by two young men, aged about 20. Evidently employees of the store, they were both busy re-arranging the six-deep arrays of bottles on the shelves. As they did so, they discussed the respective merits and drawbacks of their cars. One boasted that his tyres were still as good as new after some fantastic number of miles, the other complained that his exhaust had lasted half the time he felt he had the right to expect, and would have to spend the weekend patching it up, poor thing.

I was reluctant to interrupt this abidingly interesting dialogue, but time was short and I needed help to find the wine I had come in for. Could one of them steer me in the right direction? They did not appear particularly resentful at my enquiry, but had no idea where Argentina might be.

As I continued the search, I wondered what the average polite supermarket assistant would make of a customer's query as to the potential longevity of this or that wine. If I took a pricy 2005 claret from the shelf and asked a member of staff about its anticipated longevity, what would he or she say?

This is mere speculation – although there are plenty of super-markets selling pricy clarets these days – but my guess is that in their helpful way they would either (a) offer to ask the manager, (b) look to see if there was a back label that might give a hint or

(c) express assurances that it wouldn't have gone off yet, even though it did appear to be several years old.

OK, this is all silly. No one, surely, would fork out good money for a bottle of claret without having some idea of their own that such wines are intended for long keeping, would they? These wines are for the *educated* market. And anyone who knows their wine won't need to ask. They'll know that 2005 was the vintage of the century in Bordeaux (well, the first vintage of the century since 2000) and the grander wines will need keeping. Only the cheap ones should be broached before 2010.

In its way, claret is relatively easy to date for drinking. Although it is widely believed, and even acknowledged that the châteaux now make their wines so they mature earlier than they used to, the ten-year rule for the classed growths still holds good for decent vintages. Epic years such as 2000 and 2005 should be given longer. Thinner vintages need drinking up earlier, and if you're in doubt you can always refer to the vintage guides in diaries or the handy little cards given away by wine merchants.

My Wine Society card for 2009 tells me that Médoc and Graves reds from 2000 still need to be kept, that 1999s should be drunk and the 1998s need keeping. Going back, everything to 1993 should be drunk (with an option to give 1995 and 1996 more time) and 1992s are past their best. As to more recent vintages, while the 2004 and 2005 must be left to slumber, 2001–2003 may all be drunk now, so they say.

Of course individual wines will develop at their own pace. The top names need for ever, and as any wine merchant will admit, the ageing process can depend significantly on the conditions. Bordeaux buffs know that if they buy wine *en primeur* with a view to drinking it ten or more years after delivery, they really ought to keep it in a dark, vibration-free place where temperatures will not fluctuate too dramatically either side of 55°F (13°C).

Those with cellars under their houses need have no worries on this score. For the rest of us, there is a simple choice between rigging something up at home, or entrusting the wine to the merchant's own storage facilities, for an annual fee, for delivery when it's ready to drink. If you prefer to keep your wine under your own roof, a cupboard in a spare room might do or maybe a space in a well-insulated loft. Whatever you do, don't keep laying down wines in a kitchen or dining room, however attractive they might look in their serried racks. Heat and light will ruin your claret in far less time than it needs to reach maturity.

One option is the self-contained wine cabinet, a temperature-and-humidity-controlled box in which up to 250 bottles of wine can be stored. They can be installed anywhere that has a power supply, such as in that spare room, if there's no space in the kitchen or utility. But they cost a fortune, consume electricity and seem to me to betoken a mildly creepy sort of obsession.

While claret is the traditional *vin de garde*, there are plenty of other wines in the world made, if not for long-term keeping, then for holding on to for a bit before pulling the cork. The noble Cabernet Franc wines of the Loire and the dark monsters of the Rhône are two cases in point. Even my Wine Society card, which wants me to drink my 2001 claret and burgundy now, says I must cling on to my Rhônes a bit longer. I do believe, though, that they're talking about Châteauneuf and Cornas rather than supermarket Côtes du Rhône.

Likewise, the best Italian wines, Barbaresco and Barolo, *riserva* Chianti and those odd super-Tuscans like Ornellaia and Sassicaia need plenty of time. So do *reserva* and *gran reserva* Riojas, although the makers of these wines are gracious enough not to put them on the market until they have had an extended period in bottle, subsequent to their years in cask. It is telling, I think, that while the top

Bordeaux estates are willing to wait only a few months after the harvest to sell their wines *en primeur* and get the money in, their relatively impoverished counterparts in Spain are prepared to wait up to five years before they see any cash for their grandest wines.

Great German wines, of course, last for ever. They are the only white wines, barring stickies such as Sauternes, with any staying power. And what of the New World? Conventional wisdom has it that red wines from Australasia, the Americas and South Africa have no staying power. But this is a snooty European view that entirely misses the point.

Many good and expensive southern hemisphere wines, especially from tough grapes like the Cabernets (Sauvignon and Franc) and Syrah/Shiraz are indeed ready to drink as soon as they're released. But some of these wines will also repay keeping. Big Aussie reds do great things over a five-year span, and grand Californian wines such as those of Ridge are probably near immortal. They certainly need a good five years to reach their best.

Do cheap wines of either colour improve with age? Apparently not in the eye of the supermarkets, where most bottles seem to carry a back-label warning along these lines: 'It is recommended that this wine is consumed within one year of purchase.' For all that, it's worth hiding away a good Chilean Merlot or two, or a few Douro, Ribatejo or Alentejo reds from Portugal. Deep South French ACs such as Buzet, St Chinian, Roussillon-Villages and Madiran all have a capacity to develop in the shorter term.

And of course never neglect the maxim that even non-vintage champagne will improve noticeably if you hold on to it for a year or two. Champagne, even in the midst of economic meltdown, sells fast, and the bottles on sale in the merchants' and supermarkets might not have been there very long since their release from the *caves* in Epernay and Reims. Give them as long a rest as you can bear, and the reward should be a fuller, more rounded wine.

As to wines of great age, are they worth it? For a sense of the proverbial continuum and the unfathomable mystery of nature you can't beat the thrill of sharing an old bottle. I will never forget a supper in about 1990 in the kitchen of my friend Mario Reading. He produced a dirty old bottle of Corney & Barrow Nuits-St-Georges, which he said he'd found behind a busted fridge in the coal shed. He poured a glass for each of us. It was dark, just a little brown, with a beautiful aroma of ripe strawberries, black cherries, even something akin to roast venison. The flavour was the pure, the exuberant, the blushful, Pinot Noir. What vintage did I think? I hazarded 1976. He showed me the label. It was dated 1933.

Long live wine!

BE KIND TO SHERRY AND PORT

A great part of the pleasure in sherry is enjoying the range of aromas – from the tangy breeze of fino to the fruitcake depths of a rich oloroso. So serve sherry in a decent-sized wine glass that will allow the wine to bloom. And serve all but the sweeter 'after-dinner' types of sherry chilled. Remember, these are white wines, and as such need to be cool to bring out their freshness.

'I have no qualms about keeping all kinds of sherry in the fridge,' says George Sandeman, chairman of the sherry and port house that bears his family's name. 'It's better too cold than too warm. After all a glass will soon warm up in your hands, but lowering the temperature is much more of a problem. And because the wine will start to oxidize if you allow it to warm up in the bottle, keep it in the fridge even between glassfuls.'

Remember, too, that sherry has a finite life. The driest, palest types, fino and manzanilla, will keep at their best – in the fridge – for no more than two or three days. Dry amontillado will keep a little longer, and sweet olorosos for up to a month. George Sandeman complains that he is forever being asked for advice on 'storing' sherry: 'I tell them: when you buy it, drink it.'

Port, which has a much higher proportion of spirit than sherry, is a more stable wine. It will keep in a resealed bottle for months, but will tend gradually to go downhill.

As with sherry, drink port from a glass big enough to allow the appreciation of the aroma. A small wine glass with the classic tulip-shaped bowl is ideal. Serve white ports cold, and tawnies cool, especially as an aperitif drink.

As to decanting, the popular 'vintage character' and 'late-bottled vintage' wines are filtered before bottling so will have no deposit in them. But true vintage and 'crusted' ports that have aged many years in the bottle do need to be poured off the deposit of 'lees' that forms over time.

To decant an old wine that has been stored on its side a while, stand the bottle upright for a day to allow the lees to settle in the bottom, then uncork and carefully pour into the decanter, stopping when you see the first solids appear in the shoulder of the bottle. To get the last of the liquid, pour it through a coffee paper or muslin cloth to trap the lees, then add the clarified wine to the decanter. Old port is expensive – don't waste a drop.

TO BREATHE OR NOT TO BREATHE?

Some of us have been brought up to believe that a bottle of red wine should be opened an hour or two in advance. Others think it's pointless. My good friend and drinks-industry chemist Colin Hamilton gave me the following advice.

What happens when you open a bottle? The action merely of pulling the cork or unscrewing the cap has little if any effect, because the surface area in contact with the air is so small that very little air is dissolved into the wine. For any significant effect from aeration (exposure to air) in advance of actually pouring the wine into glasses, it needs to be decanted. Only this will allow a meaningful amount of air – and specifically oxygen – to react with the wine.

The process is called oxidation. It's a slow one, the full effects of which only become apparent after wine is left open to the air for several days or even weeks. In the end, oxidation will turn the wine into something resembling sherry. Of course this isn't the desired effect of decanting. The objective is the softening effect that occurs after an hour or so, especially in young, vigorous red wines. To explain this process calls for a short chemistry lesson.

During a wine's natural oxidative ageing process, substances such as esters and other volatiles are formed by slow chemical reaction, creating the wine's unique aroma and flavour. Also active in the wine are polyphenols, or tannins, which are described by chemists as reducing agents. In effect they quench oxygen and other oxidizing agents and thus protect the wine.

As wine ages in vat or bottle, these polyphenols condense, reacting with each other to form larger molecules. Smaller tannins take up more of the taste sites on the tongue, and thus add to the bitterness in the wine's flavour. But as the molecules condense and form larger molecules, they cover fewer receptors on the tongue and the effect of bitterness is diminished.

Instead, the effect we experience is more that of a physical coating of the tongue. It is a softer coating than the cold-tea effect of raw, newly made wine. The riper the tannins – as from, say a wine from a particularly sunny year – the softer and more pleasant the effect is. Over time, as the molecules enlarge and become insoluble, they form a sediment in the wine.

When you aerate a wine, you accelerate this ageing process by helping to release volatiles. And by encouraging a swift reaction between oxygen and tannins, the effect is to soften the wine. This action is beneficial to robust red wines, but beware of the effect on older wines. Delicate, fully mature reds in which the tannins have effectively completed their condensation reactions and have consequently thrown a deposit can be positively harmed by aeration. Oxygen can destroy the aroma and structure of an old wine at any moment, so venerable reds must be served with great care for fear of bringing their long lives to a premature end.

Delicate old reds, just like vintage ports, do very often need to be decanted off their sediments. But try to do this as gently as possible, avoiding unnecessary splashing, and serve immediately. Young reds, on the other hand, can be poured from bottle to decanter with more enthusiasm, as the intake of air will do no harm, and will almost certainly help soften the wine. And in this case, there's no need to hurry to serve the wine.

Is there any point in aerating white wines? In short, no, because whites have very little tannin. Very young whites, however, are sometimes loaded with quantities of the antioxidant-preservative sulphur dioxide, and aeration will help to disperse this pungent substance.

GASPING FOR KNOWLEDGE

The matter of letting wine breathe is hardly one of life and death, but I always enjoy quoting from a report on the topic that appeared a while ago as light relief in the medical literature. In their spare time, two distinguished doctors conducted an experiment in the hope of proving once and for all whether there is any point in opening a bottle of red wine in advance.

Dr Nirmal Charan is a pulmonologist (lung specialist) of Boise, Idaho, USA. Dr Pier Giuseppe Agostini is a cardiologist from the University of Milan in Italy. Their intention was to resolve a good-natured disagreement that arose between them over the dinner table at Dr Charan's home. The host suggested to his friend he might like to try a bottle of Idaho wine. Dr Agostini assented but suggested to Dr C. it would be a good idea to open the bottle an hour or so in advance to let it breathe.

As something of an expert in matters of respiration, Dr C. pointed out to his guest there was no scientific basis for the suggested course of action. In the proper spirit of empiricism, the two agreed that the dispute should be settled by a controlled test.

And so the following day the learned pair adjourned to Dr C.'s laboratory at the VA Medical Center in Boise, armed with five bottles of Cabernet Sauvignon. The cork of each was penetrated with a hypodermic needle and a small sample of wine taken. Each was measured for oxygen pressure in an arterial blood gas analyser, giving the reading of 30ml of mercury (as compared to 90ml in well-oxygenated human blood).

Next, the wines were opened. Further samples were taken after periods of two, four, six and twenty-four hours. For the first periods, the reading remained unaltered. Only after 24 hours had it increased significantly – to 61ml. Meanwhile, the doctors tried pouring samples from another bottle of the wine into glasses and swirling it round. After only a couple of minutes, the reading reached 150.

Dr Agostini was impressed. He returned to Milan and put his new-found wisdom to the test by inviting 35 friends to a party. He gave them all wine that had been swirled, and then wine that had been newly opened. Only two among the throng acknowledged no difference.

Then Dr A. gave the guests a 'blind' tasting of swirled and unswirled wines. To his considerable satisfaction, all but one could tell the difference, and agreed the wine tasted significantly better with aeration. He passed these results on to his friend back in Idaho. The grateful Dr Charan was able to incorporate the information into a sideshow presentation at that year's meeting of the American Lung Association in Chicago. 'Just like blood,' Dr C. told an enthralled audience of pulmonologists and thoracic surgeons, 'oxygenated wine is better than non-oxygenated wine.'

MAKING A KILLING ON CLARET

Can you make a fortune from wine? It is unlikely in the midst of a worldwide economic depression, but feasible for investors who take the long view. Wine, like equities, should be treated as a mid- to long-term investment. My own first experience in the field was vicarious. Back in 1983, I was asked by a friend working as a commodity broker in the City of London to recommend one or two of the top clarets then being offered from the 1982 vintage, the first undisputedly great Bordeaux year since 1961.

My chum was a dealer in sugar, but had several clients in the UK and abroad (notably Japan) who wished to divert some of their own money into quantities of claret, via British wine merchants. They had been reading about this 'vintage of the century' in the financial press. Tell them to buy Lafite, I advised, and suggested some reliable firms, each offering the wine at around £350 a case before duty and Value Added Tax.

Château Lafite made more than 20,000 cases of the *grand vin* in 1982, but released only a fraction of the total in the 'first tranche' put on the market. Subsequent releases from the château were made at steadily escalating prices, as the market heated up.

And heat up it did. Lafite 1982 was changing hands at £1,000 a case before the wines were bottled and delivered to customers in 1985. And in the long term, it has been a very sound investment indeed. In 2007, the twenty-fifth year after the harvest, Lafite 1982 was listed on the Live-Ex index (the wine brokers' standard price guide) at £15,000 a case before tax. The market value of the wine had multiplied by 43 times since its first release.

Consider the appreciation, tax free in the UK where wine is normally exempt from capital gains tax (see page 140). An investor who bought 30 cases of Lafite for £10,000 in 1983 could sell them for about £25,000 by 1990, £100,000 by 2000 and £450,000 in 2007. Of course there are expenses along the way: storage in the merchant's bond (a useful assurance of the wine's provenance as well as a necessary convenience) at a cost of about £200 per year, plus gently escalating insurance premiums, and a commission to a broker or saleroom of, say, 10 per cent on the sale. Over 25 years this could all add up to a hefty £50,000 but the net gain over the period would still be in the region of £400,000. It's hard to imagine any other way of turning £10,000 into that kind of money in 25 years, at least legally.

There are, I know, quite a number of wine collectors and speculators around the world who have successfully managed this coup.

But it is a rare one. Except for Château Latour, which has run Lafite fairly close, no other wine made on this scale (see page 141), including *premier cru* rivals such as Château Mouton-Rothschild and Château Cheval Blanc, has appreciated at this rate in the 1982 vintage. And no other vintage of recent times has performed, overall, as well as 1982.

Why the Lafite is valued so much more highly than other comparable wines is a mystery. American Robert Parker Jr, who became the most influential wine critic in the world largely because he raved about the 1982s, has awarded maximum points, 100, to Lafite 1982. But he has marked Mouton-Rothschild 1982 the same, and in 2009 this wine was languishing at a mere £7,800 on the price index while Lafite had climbed past £21,000. Château Latour 1982, also a 100-pointer from Parker, was running Lafite closest with a 2009 value of £12,000, but the other Médoc 1er Grand Cru Classé, Château Margaux (a meagre 98 on the Parker scale) was short of the £8,000 mark.

The lesson of the Lafite 1982 phenomenon is that tiny numbers of Bordeaux wines in very occasional vintages do perform better than their peers as long-term investments. You need luck to make a fortune. To begin with, Lafite 1982 rather lagged behind Mouton-Rothschild (though not the other three) in price inflation. By the mid-1990s, bottles of these wines were on the retail lists of grand merchants at between £200 and £500. Prices for such wines always vary outrageously between retailers, but Mouton was invariably the higher for these two until relatively recently.

Over time, tasting notes by important critics will influence the market value, and the reputations of individual châteaux do wax and wane according to events. Lafite has benefited from consistency of management since 1975 when Baron Eric de Rothschild, of the French branch of the banking dynasty, took personal control. At Mouton, Baron Philippe Rothschild, of the English branch of the family, who had bought the estate in 1922, died at the helm in 1988, bringing to an end a remarkable golden age at the estate.

An equal influence on prices is the sequence of vintages. The 1982 is still widely regarded as the best since 1961. But any subsequent year could have been nominated the 'vintage of the century' and turned investors' attention away. Luckily for speculators in the 1982, it has yet to be pipped, even by the most-hyped Bordeaux years, 2000 and 2005. In 2009, while Lafite '82 was moving serenely past £20,000 at auction, the chateau's '00 and '05 were struggling to attract bids above £8,000 and £6,000 respectively.

Wines are not immune from global trends. Although prices for top clarets from the best years were sliding less steeply than most other commodities, not to mention shares, as the economic meltdown got under way in 2008 and 2009, it is likely to be a long time before they resume the upwards trend of the preceding years. And no wine will go on rising in value forever. Unlike gold or fine art or the steadier kind of equities, all wine (Madeira excepted) is ultimately a wasting asset. Top-class claret does live long, and in a great vintage can stay in prime condition for drinking for 50 years, but after that, assuming there is any left, it can be expected to lose ground as it moves out of the sphere of drinkers and into that of the barking-mad world of historic-bottle collectors. From merchants, bottles of Lafite 1961 are commonly cheaper (if that's an appropriate word) than bottles of Lafite 1982.

Single bottles, even of the greatest wines, make dodgy investments. Only wines still in their original wooden cases, and preferably accompanied by sales receipts and storage details, will make top dollar. And only wines bought from honest merchants can be trusted. Over the last 20 years or so, numerous fraudulent 'wine investment' companies have sprung up, exploiting the greed of ill-informed speculators. At best victims are sold wines at way above market price. At worst, they pay dearly for wines that don't exist. In spite of many successful prosecutions, these criminal enterprises continue to proliferate.

It might seem entirely obvious, but only ever buy investment wines from established merchants or brokers. If they have a royal warrant, so much the better. Provenance is everything and an honest dealer should always be able to vouch for the origin of the wine. If buying wine for investment at auction, the same goes. Spurn cases without documentation.

None of this, of course, applies to wines for drinking. All good claret should be consumed long before its investment value starts to matter.

GIVE DUE WEIGHT TO CAPITAL GAIN

Wine is normally exempt in the UK from capital gains tax because the tax people regard it as just another grocery item, a 'chattel' or wasting asset as defined in section 45(1) of the Taxation of Chargeable Gains Act. But it might get complicated. As wine investment has grown into an acknowledged alternative to putting money into shares, or art, or property, questions are likely to be arising in the acquisitive minds at the Revenue. Is wine bought in quantity at a hefty price and stored in a bonded warehouse rather than in the cupboard under the proud owner's stairs really a chattel or wasting asset? The definition of 'wasting' for capital gains tax purposes is a life expectancy of under 50 years. There are plenty of wines – especially investment-type wines – that are still drinkable after 50 years, although with a very few exceptions it must be true that even the grandest wines are past their best by this age, and therefore wasting in at least one sense of the word.

The problem is that there is room for doubt, and in the

tax-collecting game, this might just be taken as an opportunity. Caution has to be the word. Any investor piling into wine must only deal with brokers or merchants whose credentials are above reproach, and whose access to current tax advice is similarly watertight.

WATCH OUT FOR THE LITTLE ONES

Three wines from tiny vineyards in the Pomerol commune of Bordeaux, Châteaux Lafleur, Le Pin and Pétrus, do regularly fetch higher prices than Lafite, but their value owes as much to rarity as to quality. None produces more than 1,000 or 2,000 cases per vintage and most are sold on an allocation basis. Early in 2009, case prices for the 1982 vintage from these estates were about £21,000, £38,000 and £32,000 respectively. Opening *en primeur* price for Château Pétrus 2006 (definitely not a vintage of the century – that title had already been given to the 2005 – but way ahead of the dismal 2007 and 2008 vintages) in the following year was £12,000.

DON'T TAKE CHANCES

The enormous increase in the value of the few wines that do have investment potential has, unfortunately, attracted the attention of chancers. Numerous companies have been set up as specialists in the field, some of them absolutely respectable, and some of them absolute robbers. The scams amount to little more than selling wines at prices very much higher than those prevailing in the legitimate trade (often by adding huge 'service' charges), or selling wines that don't exist. The premise is that the punter has no idea of the true value of the wine in the first place, let alone of its chances of rising in value, and will regard the transaction as a paper one, like a purely financial investment. The victim gets some sort of document, perhaps resembling a share certificate, and might never see the wine, because it is purported to be in storage in a bonded warehouse. In bond means the wine has not yet arrived in the UK for tax purposes, so excise duty and VAT are not payable. Telling their victims about this helps crooks defray suspicion that the wine seems to exist only on paper. Finally, when he decides to take his profits or to instruct the investment company to deliver because he wants to drink the wine, the investor gets told the value has not grown quite as projected, or that his cases have been misplaced. This is all assuming, of course, that the patsy is able to make any contact with the scamsters. They might have melted away with his money long ago.

As a journalist in wine I have had an interesting time investigating some of these dodgers, but the real ace detective in wine fraud is my old chum Jim Budd. Jim is a regular writer for the drinks trade press on the more conventional side of wine, and has written for the national newspapers. He is also the editor of *Update*, the journal (if that isn't too fancy a word) of the Circle of Wine Writers, and the author of a remarkable website, investdrinks.org, which has since 2000 exposed all manner of frauds, named names and been of material assistance to the police in bringing charges against con artists, some of whom have been convicted and imprisoned. Jim is a brave man. He has been subjected to some very unpleasant tactics by criminals, as well as legal actions of one sort or another, and has had to base his website in Canada because there are laws in the UK under which the crooks Jim exposes are allowed to lean on the internet service providers to unplug him. One wonders sometimes whose side the law is on.

With Jim's kind permission, I have extracted some germane material from **www.investdrinks.org** for this little section. I urge any reader contemplating wine investment to do nothing before having a good look through the site. Here is Jim on the matter of making a wise and considered choice not just of your merchant or broker, but of which kind of wine:

By early 2006 older vintages of Bordeaux including 1982 were starting to look considerably undervalued and when the leading Bordeaux châteaux started to demand very significant price increases for their very good 2005s prices across the board, especially for First Growths and their equivalent, prices started to rocket. This coincided with a stock market boom and a sharply increasing demand from Asia-Pacific. The rise in price for the top Bordeaux has been spectacular. However, the rise in the price of lesser fine Bordeaux has been much less spectacular as the following comparison, using wine-searcher.com between Château Latour 1996 and Château Cantemerle 1996 shows:

Latour is one of the very top Bordeaux properties, a First Growth, while Cantemerle, a Fifth Growth, is much less highly regarded. From 13 June 2004 the price of a case (12 bottles) of Château Latour 1996 rose from £1,650 (offered by Seckford Wines) to £5,400 (offered by Richard Kihl) on 26 February 2008. A remarkable gross rise of £3,750 or 227 per cent – 57 per cent per annum. In contrast on 25 May 2004 a case of

Cantemerle could be bought for £160 from Flacon Vintners. On 5 February 2008 Jakes Food & Wine were offering Cantemerle for £260 a case – a gross rise of £100 or 62.5 per cent – 15 per cent per annum. Prices are in bond, without duty and VAT.

Clearly anyone owning some Latour 1996 before the price shot up in 2006 and who had paid the right price has done extremely well. At first sight the Cantemerle owner can be reasonably satisfied. However, once wine storage charges are factored in, the position changes. Taking the storage charges (£14.38 a year or £57.53 for four), Cantemerle's increase shrinks to just 6.64 per cent a year. If prices do not continue to rise in 2008 and they may not, then the profit on the Cantemerle will be further eroded. In contrast storage charges have little effect on the Latour's recent rise. The price explosion of the past two years or so has further widened the price gulf between Bordeaux's very top wines and the second tier of the region's fine wines.

It is possible we are now at the end of this latest price jump and that we may see prices plateau over the next few years. With the credit crunch, the sub-prime crisis of late 2007/2008 allied with the weakness of the dollar and the pound's slide against the euro, the immediate future looks rocky . . . Optimists point to the demand from new markets like China and the demand for fine wine, especially Bordeaux, is far more global than ever before. We will see . . .

WINE INVESTMENT ON THE INTERNET — DON'T DO IT, MR A.

Here is a typical 2008 enquiry to Jim's website from Mr A., who has been cold-called by a company he has not previously heard of. Jim names the company on the site, but I will not do so here. 'Do you know if they are a reputable company?' Mr A. asks. 'They called out of the blue offering to sell me a case of in bond 2002 Château Lafite-Rothschild for £3,100 plus a 25 per cent £775 service charge including five years' storage charge and insurance. I'm a complete novice to wine investment, but would look to purchase some if I thought it was a good investment. My gut feeling is that although this has a Parker score of 94 and that I wouldn't be looking to sell this wine on for five years or more, the service charge is quite steep. The Decanter website offers the advice of not touching specialist wine investment companies that charge such a steep upfront commission fee. Do you think I should leave this well alone?'

Jim does indeed. He doesn't mention bargepoles, put he points out that the current price of the wine in question can be found simply by looking on the web – where one site has it at £2,600 – and that there is no reason to pay a service charge at all. If the wine were bought from a proper merchant, it could be stored for five years for under £100. And while 2002 Lafite has risen dramatically in value (from £815 in 2004) the vintage is 'unlikely to be a good long-term investment bet'.

I fervently hope Mr A. took Jim's advice.

MYSTERIOUS ORIENT

If all the millionaires who buy the first growth clarets simply held on to them for capital gain, there could, given time, be a glut. But some purchasers do buy these wines to drink. Merchants and brokers with clients in the Far East, where more and more of the most expensive names are now snapped up, report that some of their customers open the new vintages as soon as they arrive, the hallowed 2005s included. And names command little more respect than vintages.

Alan Rayne of the long-established London wine-for-investment company Magnum Fine Wine cheerfully admits he has a Hong Kong client who likes his Château Pétrus mixed with lemonade.

Whether the Chinese will sustain the fine-wine business, either as drinkers or investors, through a prolonged downturn in the US and European markets remains to be seen, but as prices slid in Western markets during 2009, wine-investment specialists were clearly hoping they would. One company, Premier Cru Fine Wine Investments Ltd, issued a press statement early in the year headlined FAR EASTERN INVESTORS SWOOP ON THE INVESTMENT POTENTIAL OF FINE WINE, AS GLOBAL EQUITY AND CAPITAL MARKETS REMAIN AT RISK. The statement reported that the favoured name is Château Lafite in a variety of vintages, but concluded in terms that must have left members of the press just a little mystified at the writer's intentions.

This is an exact transcription:

Vintages vary, with the 1st growth Lafite 1982 is the most popular depending on price, aside from this other popular vintages are 86, 96, 2000, 2003 and 2005. As you can see they are drinking some very young wines like the 03 and 05. In order for one's palette to grow and appreciate fine wine, drinking young vintages is a good place to start.

From an investment point of Premier Cru feels this will create a shortage of 03, 05's when they should be drinking as the Chinese will use them for years to come in order to learn, as usual prices should only move one way, especially with the 2005 as it is one of the great vintages.

As a rationale for investing in wine, perhaps it all makes perfect sense.

A CAUTIONARY TALE: CHÂTEAU LATOUR 1979

Bought for about £40 at Harvey's wine shop (now closed down) in Bristol ten years earlier and looked after with due care and attention, this bottle was opened in honour of a friend visiting from afar. Now 1979 was an ordinary Médoc vintage but Latour has long enjoyed a reputation for making good stuff in 'off' years. So we anticipated a treat, given its age and the nobility of its provenance. Not to mention the princely price.

Colour was most encouraging, still dense and ruby; very little browning even at the rim, and showing no sign of dilution. Nose was even better: big, ripe and 'cedary' whiff of pure, mature claret at which you could sniff happily and reflectively for a good long time.

Then we tasted it. And it was as flat as a Pauillac vineyard (think airfield). It wasn't that it was over the hill. It had clearly never lifted itself from the plain. Nor were there any signs it would do so. There was none of the famously persistent tannin of Latour to be found here, just a muddy red wine with the ghosts of a great reputation rapidly dispersing as it faded in the glass. Surely this was never a great wine. Tasted blind we believed we might have spotted it as claret, but of the supermarket special-offer variety, and unfit to drink at any price.

Latour 1979 must be scarce, which is a mercy, but there are no end of internet merchants selling odd bottles at about £150 in the wine's thirtieth year. My advice is to proceed with great caution.

COLLECTING ANTIQUE WINES

Buying very old bottles of wine is a mug's game. While exceptional vintages from the best estates might not reach their peak for drinking until 20 or 30 years old, they will almost certainly start to sicken and die by their 50th anniversaries, and need laying to rest long before their 100th.

This did not deter Christopher Forbes, an American magazine publisher, from paying £105,000 for a solitary bottle of Château Lafite 1787 at a Christie's auction in London on 5 December 1985 – that is, two years after the wine's bicentenary. The extraordinary price – the highest ever paid for a single bottle of wine, so far unsurpassed – had much to do with its claimed provenance. According to the auctioneers, it had been the property of Thomas Jefferson, the third president of the United States (1801–9), who represented the new republic as Minister to France from 1784 to 1789, and while there developed a strong interest in the wines of Bordeaux. He is known to have visited Château Lafite and other estates in the region in 1787, and to have ordered large quantities of wine for himself and his esteemed colleague George Washington.

The connection between Jefferson and the 1787 Lafite was obvious enough. His initials, Th.J., were boldly engraved immediately below the estate name ('Lafitte' in the spelling of the time) on the side of the bottle. There was also some documentary evidence of Jefferson's dealings with the estates. He preferred to buy direct rather than through wine merchants. Perhaps he was worried about fraud.

Michael Broadbent, the auctioneer, had gone to a lot of trouble to collect copies of Jefferson's correspondence, and the Christie's glass expert had confirmed the bottle was of the type in use at this period. As to where the wine had been for the last two centuries, however, remained a mystery.

The seller was a man called Hardy Rodenstock. He was a German pop music promoter already well known as a collector of rare wines. He claimed that the Lafite was one of a dozen or so bottles of similar age and also engraved with 'Th.J.' that had lately been discovered in a walled-up cellar in Paris. He had paid cash to the finder, and had not visited the location of the discovery. He did not know where it was. Rodenstock had put a reserve price on the bottle for the purpose of the auction of £5,000. This was a substantial sum. Only a handful of individual bottles had ever exceeded it.

And so to the auction. The room was packed and the bidding feverish. In £2,000 increments it reached £40,000 without pause, hesitated briefly then shook out all bidders but two by the time it hit £80,000. The underbidder, American wine magazine publisher Marvin Shanken, took it to £100,000 and later professed immense relief that Forbes decided to go one better. Afterwards, asked by the press pack if £105,000 was not an awful lot of money to pay for a bottle of wine, Forbes replied, 'It's more than a bottle of wine. It's a piece of history.'

The bottle was duly borne back to the United States where it was put on display at the Forbes museum. The lights directed on to the treasure unfortunately caused the cork to shrink and to drop into the wine. If the contents had been drinkable at any time during the previous century or two, they now certainly ceased to be so.

Other bottles from Mr Rodenstock's mysterious Paris hoard now came on to the market, and while none fetched comparable prices, they stimulated much interest in very old wines. Collecting them became high profile. Wine auctions were suddenly news, and have remained so. Then the mood began to alter. In 2005, Florida billionaire William Koch, who had bought several of Rodenstock's wines back in 1988, started an action against the German in a US Federal court alleging they were fakes. Koch claimed he had expert testimony that the engravings in the glass, similar to the Forbes prize, had been made with a modern implement, and that curators of the Jefferson museum at Monticello had been unable to substantiate the provenance of the wines.

Mr Koch, who has a collection of 35,000 bottles of wine, has subsequently initiated investigations into auction houses, retailers and individual collectors from whom he has made purchases. He is having his collection examined by experts, bottle by bottle. He has already issued other writs alleging counterfeiting. The FBI is also investigating some of the allegations. No single case has yet come to court – Mr Rodenstock does not acknowledge the jurisdiction of the Federal court – but there is every likelihood they will, in time. Whether trials will expose a network of fakery remains to be seen, but Mr Koch, a man of deep pockets and plain words, is leaving no one in doubt that he means business. 'Rodenstock is just the tip of the iceberg,' he says. 'I plan to put people in jail. I plan to get my money back, and I plan to force the auction houses and retailers to make serious changes.'

Bin Ends

Consumer surveys are notoriously unreliable, especially when it comes to getting straight answers from people about their drinking habits, but the recent (well, all right, 2005) poll conducted in Britain for Australian wine giant Hardys – then, as now, the biggest-selling wine brand in the UK – provided some entertaining insights.

Seventy-six per cent of Britons complain that the language used to describe wines, by the producers, the retailers and the media, is too pretentious. An impressive 86 per cent wish label writers would simply stick to plain English.

Nationally, 59 per cent of people claimed that wine was their favourite alcoholic drink. Only 19 per cent said beer, and likewise for spirits. Regionally, there were remarkable variations in wine-drinking habits. The Welsh spent twice as much on wine as the East Anglians. Asked to choose their favourite among red, white, rosé and sparkling, only 5 per cent in Wales nominated sparkling, compared to 37 per cent in Northern Ireland. Cabernet Sauvignon was the favourite grape for 26 per cent of East Anglians but only 3 per cent of Londoners. And so on.

The sociological aspects of the survey were mildly revealing, too. People were asked with whom they preferred to share a bottle of wine – partner, family or friends. In Scotland, only 25 per cent said partner – half the number who said so in Yorkshire and

Humberside, where there were more tête-à-tête wine drinkers than anywhere else. The Welsh were the most likely (39 per cent) and their neighbours in the North West the least likely at only 14 per cent. Scots were the most keen on drinking wine with friends (54 per cent) and Geordies (North-east), the least keen at 30 per cent.

BACK CHAT

The back labels of wine bottles are a rich source of bewildering nonsense. I particularly treasure one from Navarra. 'Palacio de la Vega represents the cutting edge of Spanish wine-making,' it raves, 'with this wine the pure intensely fruity flavours of our Tempranillo and Cabernet Sauvignon is captured by being bottled before it is put into oak barrels.'

GLITTERING PRIZE

Myths proliferate around champagne. There's the one that says it is exclusive, as it has to be made in a tightly defined region, La Champagne, north of Paris. The world's first and best sparkling wine, we are told, is also by a country mile the most expensive because the supply of the wine is limited. It cannot be increased. If demand rises – and in the long term it most certainly does in spite of occasional worldwide economic depressions – the supply cannot rise in response. Only the price can.

But the supply of champagne is in fact increasing all the time. When the first delimitation – defining of the geographical borders – of the grape-growing region took place in 1908, annual sales were about 30 million bottles. By 2008, production was edging close to 400 million bottles.

The principal explanation is that as demand for champagne has grown, more of the defined region has been planted as vineyards. Only a part of the original area was under vines, and the region was also at the time riddled with phylloxera, the dreaded beetle whose larvae destroy vines. Affected vineyards had to be grubbed up and replaced with resistant rootstocks, keeping them out of useful production for about five years.

When the *appellation d'origine contrôlée* for Champagne was finally enshrined in law in 1927, the defined zone extended to about 33,000 hectares, but of these only a third were in production, yielding between 50 and 60 million bottles a year. During the economic slump that followed, with the Second World War on its heels, the industry had a pretty flat time of it, perking up only in the 1960s when planting and replanting got under way, bringing the vineyard area to about 25,000 hectares by 1985, and the number of bottles to somewhere near 200 million.

Now the industry moved up a gear as the consumer culture of the 1980s, led by Britain – the world's leading importer of champagne – caught fire. In the intervening years, the area of Champagne planted with vines grew by 40 per cent, so that it is now very close to the maximum. With the quantity of wine that can be made per hectare of vineyard limited (though there is some wriggle room if supplies are short), it would appear that capacity is about to be reached.

In the autumn of 2007 stories started to appear in the international media about imminent rationing of champagne. Demand in India and China was spiralling upwards. The Russians, once great guzzlers of champagne but forbidden it since the Revolution of 1917, were now back in the market. There just wasn't going to be enough to go round, even though prices were escalating fast.

Time to move the goal posts. The next spate of news items revealed that the size of the Champagne AOC could, after all, be increased. The INAO, the body that regulates the appellations, confirmed that for two years it had been looking into the possibility of an extension and was considering a candidate list of up to 40 villages for addition to the existing tally of 319. The extension will not be finalized for some time, but landowners in the villages under consideration will be anxious for news. As Gilles Flutet of the INAO put it, 'If your vines lie on the wrong side of the line they will be worth 5,000 euros a hectare. On the other side, they will be worth a million.'

The myth of champagne's carefully cultivated exclusivity might have been dented, but this is surely as nought when set next to the prospect of the world's best sparkling wine actually running out.

BANG GOES THE HARVEST

English winemakers don't have it easy. Treacherous weather, punitive taxes and monopolistic supermarkets were troubles enough to Derek Pritchard of Wootton Courtenay, Somerset, who suddenly found himself facing an even more trying obstacle. One morning he awoke to find that a large number of the vines at his Dunkery Vineyard had been cut through at the stem by raiders equipped with bolt cutters.

Mr Pritchard might have incurred the wrath of villagers whose repose was being disturbed by his use of noisy bird-scaring equipment. Or he could have fallen victim to a gang of eco-hooligans from nearby Minehead or Bristol. His exchanges with neighbours had been reported in the national press, possibly stirring urban starling lovers into action.

Only English winemakers face this problem. In continental Europe, birds know better than to expose themselves to danger by attempting to steal grapes. In Burgundy I was once wandering the vineyards in the company of a convivial English-born *négoçiant* and spotted a jay. 'I don't believe I have ever seen one in these parts before,' I remarked to my companion.

'Don't suppose you have,' he said as we paused before a shot-riddled CHASSE INTERDITE sign. 'You know what they say in Burgundy: "Two Purdeys to every birdie".'

ANIMAL FLAVOURS

In a 2009 edition of *Waitrose Food Illustrated* magazine, the English illustrator Nadine Faye James was asked what kind of wine she prefers in restaurants. Her reply: 'I only order house wine. I like it best served in a giraffe.'

NOT EVEN FRENCH

The most beautiful wine château in the world is Wyken Hall at Stanton in Suffolk, England. It is home to the redoubtable American-born Lady Carla, who married into the Carlisle family in the 1980s and set about making the farm pay. She planted the seven-acre vine-yard in 1988. It produces a sparkling wine called Wyken Moonshine, among others. The Elizabethan house is sublime, altered a bit over the last four centuries (the Carlisles have been here only 100 years or so), but a lot more interesting than any of the nouveau riche nineteenth-century mock-medieval rubbish found in Bordeaux. Wyken's serious landscape gardens are open to the public and there is a posh restaurant, the Leaping Hare, as well as a shop selling the wines.

UNNECESSARY MEASURES

In the summer of 2007, swish London department store Selfridges added an interesting new wine feature. In their 'Wonder Bar' they installed an Enomatic, an automated dispensing machine that allowed customers to sample small measures of 50 interesting wines, some very grand and costing above £100 a bottle. It represented a unique chance for impecunious wine lovers to try some great names in sip-sized measures of 25ml and 75ml as well as a small-glass measure of 125ml at prices from under £1 to £30-plus.

Great idea. But not in the view of the local authority, Westminster City Council. Hearing of the juke-box-style gizmo, it sent its trading standards Gestapo in and ordered Selfridges to shut up shop. Under a 1995 amendment to the Weights and Measures (Intoxicating Liquor) Order 1988, the officials declared, wines can only be sold in quantities of 125ml, 175ml or 250ml.

Dawn Davies, sommelier at Selfridges, was forced to reset the machine to dispense no less than 125ml, with a corresponding adjustment to prices. 'It's insane,' she told trade magazine *Caterer and Hotelkeeper*. 'They stop me serving 25ml sips, but allow 250ml measures. The law is actually encouraging customers to drink more. That makes no sense.'

PURE POETRY

I am almost certain that wine writers who lapse into purple prose do so for the sheer devilry of it. Consider Morton Shand, late architect, modernist and grandfather of Camilla, Duchess of Cornwall, who wrote this in 1925: 'To compare the magnificent harmony of a fine Bordeaux to a flight of alexandrines is to pay it a doubtful compliment. Grandeur it has, and in high degree, but I find the "scansion" of Bordeaux, if scansion there must be, ranges from the Horatian to the Miltonic, from the rippling lyrics of Herrick to the sway and surge of Swinburne.'

He must have been joking. Mustn't he?

VISIT OUR CAVE

Richard Pim, a retired hydrogeologist, opens his water gardens at Pembridge in Herefordshire to the public. A feature recently added is an igloo-like dome made from 5,000 wine bottles. Their translucence bathes the resident collection of ferns in kaleidoscopic light. The bottles were contributed by friends, who have christened the attraction the Blotto Grotto.

HOSPITAL CASES

In the age of taxpayer-funded health and social security, it is tempting to believe that in earlier times, the poor were doomed to die of disease or starvation. But not necessarily so. In the centuries before the grim acquisitiveness of the agricultural and industrial revolutions in Europe, the God-fearing rich would often make wills leaving large parts of their fortunes to their parishes, in the sincere hope this might expedite their passage to Paradise.

In Burgundy, one of the most spectacular of charitable gifts made in the late Middle Ages is still very much in evidence. It is the Hôtel-Dieu in Beaune, endowed by Nicolas Rolin in 1443. He was a squire of Autun appointed Chancellor of Burgundy by the royal Valois duke, Philip the Good, at a time when the duchy was richer and more powerful than the rest of France put together.

In control of the exchequer of one of Europe's wealthiest economies, Rolin naturally accumulated a great deal of money, and decided to invest some of it in a hospital and religious foundation for the poor. Thus the world-renowned Hospices de Beaune, now a museum and tourist attraction, but still intact under its precipitous roofs, luminously tiled in the local fashion and surmounted by a host of dormer windows with gables decorated in the Flemish style.

As a hospital, the institution has been the recipient of many donations over the ensuing centuries, including a total of 131 acres of prime Burgundy vineyards. Each year, the wine from these plots (all, bar one, within the Côtes de Beaune) is auctioned, and the proceeds – as much as £2.5 million from a single vintage – invested in a state-of-the-art health centre in Beaune. Held in the spectacular council chamber, hung with priceless tapestries, the auction is held on the Sunday of Les Trois Glorieuses, the third in November.

High prices are paid by the throng of local *négociants-éleveurs* and invited guests from farther afield. In light of the good cause, it is understandable that bids are much higher than market forces would dictate. The wines, still half-formed from a harvest only a few weeks past, are very difficult to evaluate anyway. But the auction is nevertheless regarded as a useful barometer for the prices the vintage will fetch when the wines are bottled and ready for sale in the following year, or later.

Nicolas Rolin's kindness to the poor of Beaune has had a welcome spin-off for the wealthy *vignerons* of the region. Because the auction is dedicated to raising funds for charity, the community dares not allow the sums raised to fall too far below the total of the previous year. So prices, more often than not, rise – not just for the 34 wines under the Hospices de Beaune label, but for all the wines, good and bad alike, of the entire region.

In 2005, a new era began for the sale with the employment of London auctioneers Christie's to conduct the proceedings. Prices were up 11 per cent on the previous year.

THE HEIGHT OF FOLLY

Champagne and showmanship are made for each other. The firm of GH Mumm, named after German founder George-Hermann Mumm, sponsors worldwide sports including yachting and Grand Prix motor racing, and some less well-publicized events, too. One of the wildest of these took place in the summer of 2005, precisely 24,262 feet above Salisbury Plain in southern England.

It was a successful attempt to set a new world record for high-altitude dining by three young men. One of them, Bear Grylls, had conceived the idea after discovering there was an existing record for

this curious custom. It had been set by a group of climbers on a mountain somewhere. Grylls, then 31, who climbed Everest after a successful recovery from breaking his back on parachute training with the SAS, felt compelled to set a new record, but this time to do it round a table suspended from a hot air balloon.

A lunatic notion, of course, but you cannot help admiring the sheer tenacity and industry it must have taken to organize a wheeze like this. Grylls recruited the renowned adventurer and balloonist, David Hempleman-Adams, and Lt-Cdr Alan Veal, the officer in charge of the Royal Navy's Parachute Display team.

Now it was simply a matter of finding a sponsor, in the shape of GH Mumm, who provided the balloon, the refreshments and (one suspects) oodles of cash. It then required ten months' training to learn how to get a balloon four miles up into the sky with a dining table and chairs hanging below it, eat the meal (specified by the *Guinness Book of Records* at three courses, with the diners in formal dress), stay alive and get down again.

Well, they did it, and my wife – who taught the 'extremely naughty but utterly charming' Bear Grylls at his infant school – and I were among the amazed spectators at the event, safely at ground level. After parachuting back to earth, the two diners and their pilot, who landed the gigantic balloon – with its unmissable Mumm insignia – with the same weird precision on the marked spot as his colleagues had done on theirs, the team explained to us what an interesting adventure it had been.

The word surreal cropped up regularly. The temperature at 24,262 feet, they pointed out, was 45 degrees below zero, and the meal – of asparagus spears, duck and fruit salad all served from a 'warm box' – had to be eaten between intakes of oxygen.

They needed to take some peculiar precautions. 'You had to be very careful not to drop any of the asparagus,' said Lt-Cdr Veal. 'If a spear went over the side, it would certainly kill anyone four miles below unlucky enough to get under it.'

There was, naturally enough, a bottle of Mumm champagne firmly attached to the table. But I fear the diners must have had to pass on a glassful. At minus 45 degrees, the wine would be frozen beyond recognition.

I asked the nice lady from Mumm why they had sponsored the whole thing in the first place. She told me it was part of Mumm's salute to the fiftieth anniversary of the Duke of Edinburgh Awards in that year, and that anyway the whole thing had seemed a good idea at the time. For myself, I would also like to think the reasoning behind this kind of sponsorship is that adventures and champagne have a certain amount in common. You don't participate in either because it's virtuous or improving.

A SECRET FOR WINE DRINKERS — WORLD'S BEST WINE TOWN

Wine towns are often tourist towns, and this is certainly true of Sanlucar de Barrameda. But it is a Spanish resort, not (yet) an international one. In particular, it is a retreat for the people of Seville, the greatest city of Andalucia, 50 miles inland. I have visited the town a number of times since a first trip in 1988 with David Sandeman, then head of the famous sherry shippers, on a works outing from the Sandeman bodegas in Jerez. My excuse was that I was writing the bicentenary history of the company, and this outing would provide an excellent opportunity to get better acquainted with

the people who grow the grapes and make the wines.

Our destination was the Casa Bigote, which I was assured was the best fish restaurant in Andalucia. It stands on the beach, amid a kilometre-long strand of rather tumbledown buildings resembling a boardwalked street in the Wild West. It faces directly on to the vast expanse of golden sand that forms Sanlucar's shore with the Atlantic estuary of the Guadalquivir River. Into the Bigote we piled, in the early evening light, to begin a heroic session of sampling sherries and *tapas*, then a new phenomenon to me. We must have consumed dozens of these little meaty and fishy snacks, and downed a great number of ice-cold *copitas* of Sandeman's finos and numerous manzanillas too, before to my astonishment it was announced, not long before midnight, that it was now time for dinner.

This is how it is in Sanlucar. It was only years later that I discovered the town proper, on a visit to the leading local producer Hidalgo, whose bodega is in its very centre. The old town is made up of little plazas latticed with a few avenues and many narrow winding lanes punctuated by baroque churches, dignified houses, even a palace or two.

Sanlucar is not at all a resort like Malaga or Marbella on the Mediterranean 100 or so miles round the coast to the east. It's a Spanish town. Nobody here walks the elegant streets in swimwear. There are no facilities laid on for foreign tourists. If you wish to be served in the market, the shops or the teeming bars and restaurants, you must speak whatever Spanish you can muster. Britain is the best export customer for the town's sublime sherries, but few here speak a word of English.

Beach life in Sanlucar has its quirks. Unusually for a seaside town, most of the best restaurants and tapas bars are, like Casa Bigote (still Andalucia's finest), right on the beach, which stretches an impressive distance, easily 100 metres, to the sea, and then for many miles up the coast. This must be the only beach in Spain, maybe in Europe, that is simply incapable of becoming overcrowded.

And it is the venue of one of the world's most extraordinary equestrian events, the Carreras de Caballos. At the height of the holiday season in August, thoroughbred racehorses ridden by professional jockeys compete in a series of hair-raising sprints along the waterline. There are two meets during the month, each of several days, and the races are staged in the evening, the last just as the sunsets.

It is the kind of occasion that could simply never happen in Britain. The few metres of sand running down to the water are cordoned off with builders' tape and amiable policemen take up position on the course to discourage the thousands of spectators from wandering into the path of the race as the start is awaited. But the tape is soon trampled underfoot and as soon as the horses come into view down the curve of the beach, the crowd presses perilously forwards. The animals, up to eight abreast, flash by at terrifying speed, almost within touching distance of the shrieking punters.

It is a wonderfully exciting spectacle, comparable with the Palio of Siena but without the pomp. There is manic betting in the enclosure (where Sanlucar high society turns out dressed as if for Ascot) and also at little stalls all along the beach, run by children. They scratch a line in the sand opposite their pitch and offer odds on which runner will cross it first. How the placings can be put beyond dispute is an utter mystery. The Jockey Club would not approve.

Lack of regulation, but civilized order, are both marks of this wonderful town. As nanny-state Brits, we were nostalgic to see motorcycle riders of all ages without crash helmets, and young children free to roam the centre far into the night. The hours kept here are very Spanish, with the main square, the Plaza de Cabildo, still packed with families enjoying coffees and *helados* from the ice cream parlour in the square, and last suppers well into the small hours.

The plaza, with centrepiece fountains and an enormous palm at each corner, is surrounded on all four sides by bars whose massed terrace tables fringe the entire perimeter. It's a square small enough to be intimate, but sufficiently large to provide promenading room for the young, all dressed in their finest, to pass to and fro in that indispensable Spanish pursuit of admiring and being admired. The enclosing three-storey eighteenth-century buildings are discreetly lit, turning the whole scene into pure theatre.

Most of the bars have one thing in common with British pubs – they are *autoservicio*, meaning that you place your order over the counter. On our visits my wife Sheila and I have learned to shriek imploringly through the scrum at the bar for manzanilla or *cerveza* (beer – there's only one make, a lager called Cruzcampo) and then, having got the barman's attention, go through the routine of ordering universal tapas such as *gambas* (prawns) and *langostinos* (huge prawns).

The seafood here might well be the best in the world. It is, remember, a cold-water Atlantic port, not a warm Mediterranean one. At the Casa Bigote, which we have long since come to know well, you choose on the basis of the catch of the day. It's all laid out fishmonger-style for inspection, and you choose not just your fish, but how you'd like it cooked. The bream we had on the last occasion in the local method, baked whole with potatoes and garlic and served straight from a baking tray placed on our table, remains the most perfect fish dish of our memories.

But it's not entirely about fleshly pleasures. Sanlucar is a very ancient place with history in depth. It was founded by the Phoenicians – Syrian seafarers – about 400 BC. Subsequently colonized by the Romans, the Visigoths and then the Moors, it was the major seaport of the region by the time of Spain's sixteenth-century Golden Age.

It was from Sanlucar that Columbus and other ruthless adventurers set off to pillage the Americas.

The legacy of all this is a treasury of architecture from the Morisco period onwards. There are sublime churches decorated with spectacular ornament. If you like your crucifixions explicit, this is the place for you. And there is even a lovely Anglican church built here during the reign of Henry VIII for the benefit of the many English merchants then in Sanlucar for the sherry trade.

There is the palace of the Medina Sidonia family, now a civic building and open to visitors. A duke of Medina Sidonia commanded the disastrous Armada against England in 1588, but the family survived this setback and is still regarded as the first dynasty in these parts.

One of the unmissable attractions lies on the other side of the estuary. It is the Doñana National Park, a vast wild delta region lately rescued from planned development for farmland and housing. This pristine landscape of marsh and woodland hosts resident and migratory birds in great profusion, and was saved from the bulldozer largely thanks to Javier Hidalgo of the sherry company. He combines winemaking with horse racing (he has often competed at Sanlucar) and serious ornithology. The Doñana Park is one of Europe's great nature reserves – lynx, wild boar and other endangered mammals roam it – and you can take organized tours by four-wheel-drive or riverboat from Sanlucar. You will be looking at landscape of an unspoiled kind now almost entirely lost to Europe.

Sanlucar itself has been a lost place for several centuries, superseded in the 1600s by Seville as a mercantile centre and simultaneously by Cadiz, just along the bay, as a seaport. For the last 200 years, the town has been getting by on fishing and local tourism, and from the new life injected into its wine trade by the pale and tangy manzanilla style that was devised here in the early 1800s.

But don't expect the town to remain undiscovered for much longer. Resort developments are now being built behind the beaches nearby, and the reputation of the local wine and seafood is starting to attract gastronomic travellers from outside Spain. The secret will soon be out.

DESERT ISLAND WINES

In the early days of *Desert Island Discs*, castaways on the BBC Radio programme's sequestered isle commonly chose wine as their luxury. Château Lafite was a popular choice in the 1950s and 1960s, with Alfred Hitchcock and Gregory Peck among the memorable nominators, and champagne received an encouraging number of requests.

The great barrister-author Sir John Mortimer (1923–2009), who featured a record three times on the programme, wanted champagne on his first appearance. He was never ashamed to admit that he liked to drink champagne every day, starting at breakfast if possible. But he mused that he would not be able to get enough on the island, and opted instead for a bath. He got all his ideas for stories while bathing, he explained. Presenter Roy

Plomley, in a moment of inspiration that pleased Mortimer greatly, had the bright idea of filling the bath with champagne for him.

But as the political correctness of the 1980s gathered momentum, celebrities proved diminishingly willing to air their personal drinking preferences. Wine and other alcoholic drinks dried up. Curiously, in spite of the continued tightening of the puritan grip, castaways have more recently been throwing caution to the winds. In 2005, artist Maggi Hambling demanded the entire wine cellar of All Souls and in the following year jockey Frankie Dettori weighed in with a request for a lifetime's supply of Pinot Grigio. In 2007, Irish novelist Edna O'Brien was all for a 'vault of very good wine' and scholarly writer on religion Karen Armstrong prayed for a continuing supply of cold, white wine. Veteran journalist Katharine Whitehorn's plea was less particular: a machine to distil whatever on the island could be turned into alcohol. Brand names were back in 2008, when West End musical star Michael Ball called for a supply of New Zealand's famed Cloudy Bay Sauvignon Blanc.

AT THE MOVIES

Wine has had its moments in cinema. *Sideways*, the unexpected comedy hit of 2005 filmed amid the vineyards of California, has certainly proved that the theme can work. The huge box-office success of the film even had an incidental impact on US sales of red wines. Demand for Pinot Noir ('its flavours are just the most haunting and ancient on the planet') soared, and interest in Merlot ('If anyone orders Merlot, I'm leaving') plummeted in line with melancholy hero Miles' forcefully expressed convictions.

This side effect might be what convinced the producers to go ahead with the 2008 movie *Bottle Shock*. It is the tale of the triumph of Californian wines over their French counterparts in a competitive tasting that took place in Paris in 1976. Based on real events and focusing on Chateau Montelena in the Napa Valley, which supplied the six-dollar Chardonnay that outpointed priceless Bâtard-Montrachet, Meursault and Beaune Clos des Mouches from Burgundy, the film makes a splendidly one-sided case for Californian wine.

The Montelena story is an authentically romantic one. Founded in 1882, the estate was extinguished by Prohibition in 1919 and made no more wine until it was bought in 1968 and replanted by a group of people including lawyer Jim Barrett. The first vintage to go on sale was the 1972 and it was the Chardonnay of the following year that triumphed in the Paris tasting. In the movie, the stars are Jim Barrett, played by Bill Pullman (the President in sci-fi blockbuster *Independence Day*) and his surfer son and successor in the business Bo, played by Chris Pine, who subsequently starred as Captain Kirk in 2009's *Star Trek* feature.

The principal appeal for audiences in Britain, where *Bottle Shock* was released in 2009, has probably been that Steven Spurrier, the toffee-nosed English wine merchant who set up the Paris tasting, is portrayed by national treasure Alan Rickman. It is an anachronistic piece of casting as Rickman was past his sixtieth birthday by the time he was filming the role, and Spurrier was only 34 back in 1976. Spurrier has described the film's portrayal of him as 'false, defamatory and disparaging', but has shown hints of seeing the funny side. Complaining that he had been made to appear 'impossibly effete' he conceded that at the time he might have been effete, but not impossibly so.

Bottle Shock's director, Randall Miller, gave a nice preamble to the project:

So why a wine film? It's all about these characters – these people are amazing. The first time I went to Chateau Montelena to meet Bo Barrett, he was on the phone in his office. He's about 50. I listened as he turned down Sotheby's on some huge event in his honour. When I asked him why did he turn them down, Bo replied, 'Sniffin' and spittin', nah, I'd rather be on a beach in Cabo drinkin' rum outta a coconut.' Arguably one of the greatest winemakers of our day, Bo is a guy I could immediately relate to, and not just for his appreciation of exotic journeyman beverages. Immediately after I left I called Jody, my wife and creative partner, and said we have to do this film. If it wasn't for the Barretts, and people like them, with a dream to make wine to rival the French, the California wine industry would never have exploded. It was a story that needed to be told.

Randall Miller's wife Jody Savin, the producer of *Bottle Shock*, is convinced that the Paris tasting was a turning point not just for Californian wines but for the entire industry worldwide:

Growing up, my parents drank California wine. It was Almaden and it came in a box with a bladder and a little plastic spigot on the side. It was cheap. When company came over, the California wine stayed hidden in the laundry room. It wasn't chic and it wasn't good. No, when company came over, they drank French wine. My parents had no idea that Jim Barrett and Warren Winniarski and others like them were pursuing a dream of making great wines in California at the time.

I clearly remember though that there was a moment when that all changed – when it suddenly became interesting to drink California wine. It wasn't Almaden in a box or a juglike bottle with a convenient handle on its side. It was good wine, new wine, inspired wine and we no longer hid it in the laundry room. But I never knew what triggered that change until I heard the story of *Bottle Shock*.

The now-famous Paris wine tasting of 1976 began as the notion of a British wine shop owner in Paris. It was a minor event really. Designed to engineer some publicity for the man's wine shop. But what happened at that minor event had major repercussions. The French went into that tasting expecting a slam-dunk. It is understandable. Up until that moment pretty much everyone in the world subscribed to the chauvinistic belief that great wine could only be cultivated in the hallowed *terroir* of the French wine country. California vintners today talk about 'Before Paris' and 'After Paris'. There is no doubt that the results of that Paris tasting triggered the democratization and the globalization of the wine industry.

LOST COS

The French came within a short distance of avenging themselves on Chateau Montelena in 2008, when Château Cos d'Estournel, one of the great estates of Bordeaux, made an offer for the Napa Valley property. Although it was widely reported at the time *Bottle Shock* was on release in the US that more than $100 million had changed hands in what Montelena owner Jim Barrett called 'a dream marriage', the deal in fact had withered on the vine by the winter. Worldwide financial chaos was, inevitably, blamed.

FORTHCOMING ATTRACTION

Another film based on the 1976 tasting saga, tentatively entitled *The Judgment of Paris*, might follow *Bottle Shock*. It is based on a book of that name written by James Taber, then of *Time* magazine, who happened to be the only journalist present at the great event itself.

What made the outcome of the tasting particularly painful for French winemakers was that most of the judges were French, and all very senior members of the trade. They included the head of the INAO, the regulator of the Appellations d'Origine Contrôlée, Aubert de Villaine of the Domaine de la Romanée-Conti, Pierre Tari, owner of Château Giscours and secretary of the Bordeaux Association des Grands Crus Classés, along with the head sommelier from Paris' legendary La Tour d'Argent and the owners of two more leading restaurants. The tasting was 'blind' so that none of the wines were identified in advance, and while California's Montelena Chardonnay came in ahead of all the burgundies, the winning red was Stag's Leap Cabernet Sauvignon 1972, pipping respectively Châteaux Mouton-Rothschild, Haut-Brion and Montrose, all from the 1970 vintage.

It was unquestionably a fair cop. The good name of Californian wine was deservedly boosted, and the French simply had to bear the humiliation at what was already a pretty bleak time following a long line of appalling vintages in both Bordeaux and Burgundy, and a major fraud scandal in Bordeaux in 1975. Steven Spurrier certainly won himself a lot of publicity, but little if any in France, where a chauvinistic media kept very quiet about the shock results.

Spurrier still works in the wine trade and is an admired writer on the subject. It is to his credit that he restaged the 1976 event with thirtieth-anniversary tastings of the same red wines (the whites were all gone, in one sense or another) in both the US and France. The

2006 results left no room for doubt. Out of the ten wines entered, the judges put five of the six Californians in the first five places. Mouton-Rothschild 1970, placed second in 1976, this time came sixth.

GRANT CRU

The actor Hugh Grant was characteristically self-effacing in an interview with the Bordeaux wine trade's in-house magazine. Did he consider himself a connoisseur, they asked. 'All I know I learned from the Sainsbury's book of wine,' confessed Grant. 'But I did feel quite smug at a wine-tasting dinner in Los Angeles the other day, when I was the only one of 20 guests who could spot the Australian Syrah among the first growth Médocs.'

And where, and with whom, did he most enjoy drinking wine? 'Lunchtime is my favourite time. And preferably with Californians since it's fun to see how shocked they are.' Any particular favourite wines? 'A bit lowbrow. Provençal rosé, for example. I also adore top white burgundies and fab clarets, but I always think these taste better if someone else is paying for them.'

DELIVERY BY SAILING SHIP

In 2008, Frédéric Albert launched a new wine-transport service for producers in the region of Languedoc in south-west France. The Compagnie de Transport Maritime à la Voile (CTMV) operates a 170ft three-masted barque, the *Belem*, out of Bordeaux, on routes to Dublin and London. The ship, built in 1896 for the chocolate trade with Brazil and unreliably reported to be the last sail-powered merchant vessel ever built in France, carries up to 5,000 cases of wine, and returns with crushed recycled glass for the Bordeaux bottle industry. M. Albert said that the maiden voyage to Dublin had saved more than eight tons of carbon.

'The idea is to do something for the planet, and something for the wines of the Languedoc,' he declared, adding that his interest in the venture was inspired by his grandfathers, one a winemaker, the other a sailor. The CTMV aims to build a fleet of seven sailing vessels and to extend the routes across the Atlantic. M. Albert will deal only with wine producers who follow the principles of sustainable viticulture, and is keen that inland transport to the port of Bordeaux should exploit the Canal du Midi and other waterways of south-west France.

Bottles of wine shipped this way are labelled with the legend 'Carried by sailing ship – a better deal for the planet.'

A HEALTH WARNING WITH EVERY BOTTLE

It prevents the common cold; it reduces the risk of cancer and heart disease; it stimulates creativity; it enhances memory; it prolongs life. It increases the risk of cancer and heart disease, and causes cirrhosis of the liver; it shrivels the sexual organs; it diminishes creativity and memory; it brings about madness and premature death.

All these assertions have been made about the effects of alcohol in general, and sometimes about wine in particular. All have been nominated in the conclusions to scientific studies carried out, at public expense, in recent years.

The paradoxical nature of the results is surely simply explained. The ill effects are attributable to alcohol abuse; the benefits are derived from moderate drinking. Booze is an agreeable servant, but a cruel master, etc. But the reporting of research is not guaranteed to be balanced. Data that demonizes alcohol is leaped upon by voluble lobby groups. Studies showing inconclusive results or even suggesting that responsible drinking is harmless are not reported at all. The drinks industry is forbidden by law to make any claims whatsoever for its products.

The media, on the other hand, invariably likes to make a big splash of every new report into the dangers of drink – preferably on an apocalyptic note. When doctors in Britain reveal to a Department of Health inquiry that some of their patients regularly drink a bottle of wine with their supper, the *Daily Telegraph* gets to hear about it and warns there is to be a 'Crackdown on middle-class wine drinkers'. When one in twelve alcoholics questioned in a poll admits to a loss of libido, the *Sun* cannot resist a memorable headline: DRINK'LL WRINKLE YOUR WINKLE.

Wine lovers who look forward to a glass or two with their evening meal might believe they can observe all this irrelevance from a safe distance. But now they are told by a health minister that they are 'middle-class binge drinkers' endangering their health by exceeding the Government's 'Sensible Drinking' guidelines.

What none of us is likely ever to hear from a health

minister, and even less likely to hear from the media, is that drinking wine in moderation is not injurious to health and might very well be beneficial to it. And it is harder still to visualize any member of the medical profession venturing into this territory, even on the firm ground of red wine and cardiovascular health.

Heart disease is the principal cause of death in the Western world, and there may well be physicians who would like to mention to anxious, at-risk patients that taking a glass of red wine has not only useful sedative effects, but is known in many cases to raise the levels of high-density lipoproteins (HDLs) in the blood. The doctor could explain that an increased level of these lipids in proportion to low-density lipoproteins (LDLs) significantly improves the prognosis for some heart patients. But while the doctor might prescribe drugs and/or lifestyle changes, he or she will not be playing the role of sommelier. It just doesn't go with the job description.

Scientific journals regularly report trial evidence of benefits from moderate drinking, and some of these do find their way into the public domain. Oft quoted is the French study in which volunteers drank 50cl of red wine daily for two weeks. Their HDLs were measured before and after, and showed significant increases. The volunteers then switched for a similar period to the same quantity of alcohol, but taken in other forms, including white wine. This time there was no change in HDL levels. The difference, the researchers reported, lay in the presence of resveratrol, a fungicidal organism present on grape skins. Resveratrol is abundant in red wine simply because the grape skins are included in the fermentation.

This study and others have fuelled a fashion in the United States for drinking red wine, an effect which has, as these things do, gradually taken hold in Britain. The long-standing ratio of two-thirds white wine to one-third red that characterized the UK market from the year dot had by 2008 moved very close to half and half (with rosé rising fast), at the same time as wine sales reached a new peak overall.

Increases in sales of any kind of alcohol are, however, invariably greeted with admonitory gloom by health lobbyists. The British Medical Association has continually demanded higher duties on alcohol, calling for warning labels on bottles and cans and mandatory public notices advising of the dangers of drink in pubs, bars and restaurants. And the BMA is getting its way. Under a new government code of practice, measures of this kind are being introduced throughout the licensed trade in 2010. All pubs, bars and restaurants will be compelled to offer small 125ml glasses – once universal but long since displaced by the 175ml glass as standard – to customers requesting wine.

One political philosopher, the libertarian economist Ralph Harris – elevated to the peerage as Lord Harris of High Cross – had a trenchant view of this sort of activity. Its purpose, he said, was 'to spread fear, to discredit private enterprise, and so to justify state intervention'.

Lord Harris, who died in 2006 aged 81, might have extrapolated too far, but at least he had the courage to speak his mind. He would no doubt have agreed with the sentiments of an earlier philosopher on the matter of alcohol. This was Socrates, in the fourth century BC: 'Wine lubricates and calms the spirits, revives joy and is oil to the dying flame of life. If we drink temperately, a little at a time, the wine is as sweet morning dew to our senses. This way, it will not steal our reason, but gently coaxes us to congenial mirth.'

WINE — THE BEST MEDICINE

When Frenchman Michel Montignac worked as an executive in the pharmaceutical industry, he put on weight thanks to too many business lunches. Concerned about this, he devised his own method of countering the effect, and improving well-being generally. He described it all in a 1986 book called *Dine Out and Lose Weight* and has since become a bit of a diet guru. But it is his first masterpiece that is my bible, and the section I treasure most deals with the benefits of particular wines in the treatment of common ailments. I have never fathomed the connections between the conditions and the cures, but would not for a moment doubt M. Montignac's sincerity.

For those unfamiliar with his work, let me pass on a few tasters:

> For asthma – Corbières.
> For constipation – white Anjou and Bergerac.
> For depression – Chablis.
> For gout – Provence rosé.
> For menopause – red burgundy.
> For obesity – Alsace.
> For old age – Aloxe Corton.
> For arteriosclerosis, flu, gout, old age,
>   rheumatism and tuberculosis – champagne.

M. Montignac counsels 'you should drink no more than half a litre a day' of the prescribed wine and that 'one glass of wine at the end of the meal is enough to benefit from the drink's therapeutic properties'.

WORTH REMEMBERING

Three glasses of red wine per day improve memory and stave off the onset of neurodegenerative diseases such as Alzheimer's, according to Professor Alberto Bertelli of Milan University, who has conducted many years of research with human volunteers. The

effect, he says, is due to resveratrol, a polyphenol present in grape skins, which lowers levels of the amyloid-beta peptides blamed for laying down the plaque associated with Alzheimer's.

TEMPS PERDU

'*Pas plus d'un litre par jour*' – advisory slogan on wine consumption by French health minister Pierre Mendès-France in the 1950s.

'It has been scientifically proven that wine kills the bacterium that causes typhoid fever in a matter of minutes' – Gaston Derys in *Mon Docteur le Vin*, 1936, republished by Yale University Press, 2004.

OVERDOING IT

In its 'Sensible Drinking' guidelines, the UK's Department of Health recommends that a weekly 'safe limit' for alcohol consumption is 21 to 28 units for men and 14 to 21 for women. A unit is 8 grams or 1 centilitre of ethanol (pure alcohol) and equates to a small measure of table wine, about 120ml, half a pint of ale or a pub serving of spirits. The present levels were introduced in 1995, extending the previously unequivocal 21 and 14 units. These had been announced in 1987. Before then, the safe limit had been the same for men and women – 56 units per week.

HOW MUCH IS ENOUGH

Drinking regular, moderate quantities of alcohol in general, and red wine in particular, prolongs life and improves health. There are probably many objective medical practitioners, and policymakers in health matters, who believe this. But of course no member of the profession, or politician, dares to advocate the consumption of alcohol.

Neil Stone, chairman of the nutrition committee of the American Heart Association, has put the establishment case succinctly: 'Wine can't be recommended as a public health measure because of those who can't control their drinking.' There you have it. Official endorsement of the benefits of a glass of wine would promote alcohol addiction. But governments go further. Not only do they avoid recommending drinking; they work hard to suppress evidence that alcohol is beneficial, even in moderation.

Why do they do this? A few years ago, I heard an explanation at a memorable conference in London on the topic of wine and health.

Andrew Barr, a rather controversial writer on the sociology of wine and the only non-medical speaker on the day, put it this way:

Health officials are wedded to a statistical theory known as the Ledermann hypothesis after the French statistician who formulated it that any increase in average alcohol consumption automatically leads to an increase in alcohol-related problems. Once you know the Ledermann theory you can understand why the World Health Organization has adopted a policy of telling everybody to cut down his drinking, however moderate, and has promulgated the motto 'Less is Better' and why the UK government has a policy of 'sensible drinking limits', telling everyone to keep his consumption below a certain arbitrary level. We should cut down our consumption, not so much for our own sake, as for the sake of the country at large.

Obviously, the Ledermann theory is wrong. The harm caused by alcohol depends more on the context in which it is drunk than on the quantities consumed. Someone who drinks half a bottle of spirits on a Saturday night but nothing during the week is likely to cause more harm to himself and others than another person who consumes the equivalent quantity of alcohol over the course of a week, spread out in the form of a quarter of a bottle of wine each day with meals. Yet if the first person converts from drinking his half-bottle of spirits in a binge to sipping wine with food on a regular basis but consumes slightly more overall, say a third of a bottle of wine a day then, according to Ledermann, he will be contributing to an increase in alcohol-related problems in his society. It is because of this nonsense that we are all told to cut down on our drinking and the results of research into the benefits of moderate alcohol consumption are suppressed.

And just how convincing is that research? Judging by the evidence presented at the conference, it is incontrovertible. The key word is antioxidants. These are plant-derived chemicals found on vegetables and fruits. They slow the rate at which plants degenerate as a result of exposure to oxygen and if we eat or drink these antioxidants they have similarly beneficial effects for us. Happily, antioxidants live in abundance on the skins of grapes, and in the process of being turned into wine their benefits are actually enhanced.

Dr Thomas Stuttaford, born in 1931 and still a medical writer for *The Times*, was among the speakers. A fearless proponent of moderate drinking, he addressed the topic of antioxidants and was admirably lucid:

Why are antioxidants so valuable? Without oxygen we wouldn't survive. Oxygen is essential for life, but paradoxically oxygen is toxic. Look at some wrought-iron gates which have stood for centuries in front of a stately home. Provided that the metal is protected by red lead and paint from the oxygen in the atmosphere, they won't rust. Let oxygen get at the metal and they are destroyed in a few years. Likewise, human beings are sensitive to the toxic effects of life-giving oxygen. We don't have red lead to protect us, but instead the antioxidants which are part of a complex defence mechanism against the ill effects of oxidation, keep us alive.

Over the years, the oxidation processes contribute to many of the degenerative, and probably malignant diseases. We may not mind our hair going grey, but it is more alarming if our arteries become clogged with atheroma, the porridgy, fatty material which clings to the inside of the artery and therefore leads to heart attacks, strokes and high blood pressure, and we would very much rather do without the malignant diseases.

The oxidation process attacks and damages the DNA, the core of the cell. The average human cell experiences 10,000 oxidative hits to its DNA each day; the protective enzymes neutralize most of this damage but not unfortunately all of it. The amount of damaged DNA accumulates with age and, as it does so, so does the risk of cancer. Antioxidants may not only prevent malignancies starting, but some think they may inhibit their development and possibly even cause regression of any carcinogenic process. Of 156 dietary studies of cancer at sites other than the prostate, 128 demonstrated that cancer risk was reduced by a high antioxidant intake. Since these studies have been completed, amazing figures for the beneficial effects of the antioxidant lycopene, found in tomatoes, have been found. Ten helpings of tomato juice a week will *halve* the incidence of cancer of the prostate.

Dr Stuttaford spoke in a wonderfully unstuffy way about these serious matters and seemed to relish the task of broadcasting material some of his colleagues would rather we didn't hear. 'Wine is good for you in moderation and sometimes not even in moderation,' he said with mischievous glee, 'although it is of course a very closely guarded secret in which ways.'

One of these ways is connected with the aforementioned atheroma, which builds up in the arteries when blood fats known as low-density lipoproteins (colloquially known as 'bad cholesterol') displace high-density lipoproteins ('good cholesterol') in the bloodstream. A diet high in the antioxidant resveratrol has been shown conclusively to help maintain the right balance between the two. And resveratrol is abundant on the skins of grapes used in winemaking. Dr Stuttaford took a robust view of the best method of preventing atheroma build-up: 'If you can inhibit this process by drinking half a bottle of claret every night, what better treatment could there be?'

According to another speaker, Dr Denis Blach of Dijon University's Medical School, there is absolutely no doubt left that antioxidants in general and the flavonols (including resveratrol) in particular are vital in preventing heart disease. An example he gave was platelet aggregation – the tendency for blood fats to stick together and form the clots that cause thrombosis. Experiments have shown that introducing resveratrol into the bloodstream of coronary patients reduces the risk of aggregation from a factor of 88 per cent to a factor of 10 per cent.

And which wines deliver this resveratrol? 'I wouldn't like to feed the war between the regions by revealing the details,' Dr Blach told us diplomatically, 'but the winemaking process is perhaps more important than the region. Maceration is vital.' He meant that red wines made from must in which the skins have steeped for long periods are likely to be the best.

This was the finding of a Glasgow University research programme which found that Cabernet Sauvignon from the Lontue region of Chile was number one. Other studies, though, have found that cooler regions, including Bordeaux and Burgundy, also produce high resveratrol levels, because they need to steep their grapes longer for maximum extract. Very high levels of up to 30mg, said Dr Blach, have been measured in some Burgundy Pinot Noir reds. For comparison, note that white wines typically contain less than 1mg of resveratrol.

It was a long and detailed seminar, in which a large audience was left in no doubt about the close connection between drinking moderate quantities of red wine and improved health. Some astounding assertions were made: risk of cancers and Alzheimer's disease are both significantly reduced in people who drink red wine. The risks from alcohol (addiction, liver damage, raised blood pressure) are outweighed significantly by the benefits.

It was a daring seminar, too. Dr Stuttaford touched on blood pressure and alcohol: 'Even if you have only three drinks a day your systolic blood pressure can be marginally raised. This is a transitory effect and marginal. Giving up drink is very unlikely to improve your survival. Giving up alcohol is unlikely to compensate for the loss of benefit.' Commenting on a report that the risk of Alzheimer's disease could be reduced by drinking wine, Dr Stuttaford, then 68, rounded the day off in robust style: 'Drinking wine means a longer life and a *saner* life. There's no good living to my age or ten years older if you're going to be totally gaga.'

HOW TO GET TO 90

Film producer William MacQuitty (1905–2004), who witnessed the departure of the *Titanic* in 1912 and made the classic 1958 movie of the ship's loss, *A Night to Remember*, wrote a book called *How to Reach Ninety and Make the Most of It*. Part of his formula, as befitted the ancestor of Jane MacQuitty, wine correspondent of *The Times*, was to drink a daily half-bottle of claret.

LONG LIFE

Frenchman Pierre Galet is one of the world's leading ampelographers – vine scientists – and a sincere believer in the healthy effects of drinking wine. At the inauguration of the Centre d'Ampélographie Alpine at Cevins in Savoie, France, in 2007, Professor Galet declared among many other things that he enjoys wine with every meal and drinks 365 bottles a year except in leap years, when he drinks 366. Professor Galet was born in 1921.

The Last Drop

BUCKING THE TREND

Connoisseurs of wine are found in all sorts of places. In Scotland, perhaps unexpectedly, there is a following for a brand that hails from England. Buckfast tonic wine is made at a Benedictine abbey in Buckfastleigh, Devon. It is a sweetened and flavoured potion from French grape must fermented to 15 per cent alcohol. To the reported dismay of the monks, who have been making it since 1880, Buckfast is the preferred libation among young street drinkers, locally known as 'neds' in the Lanarkshire town of Coatbridge and other urban centres. The drink has been blamed for causing social disorder by politicians including Andy Kerr, Health Minister in the Scottish Parliament, who described it as 'seriously bad'. There was, he recently declared, 'something different about that drink that does something to our young people'.

Buckfast devotees appear to agree with him. Reports on the drink posted by enthusiasts on Scottish websites have included these:

> Buckfast is a great wee drink.
> Terry Wogan drinks Buckfast. That's how good the stuff is! Pure necter.
> Sittin here chillin after a heavy night at the dancin, had ma buckie in the fridge waiting for me to come home can't beat a nice chilled bottle of vino to bring u round eh? Popeye had his spinach, the gummiebears had their gummie berry juice and God bless those monks for bringin us buckfast tonic wine!
> Bucky's pure gemm inawaeeerat. Loogit pam's chickly gels. Loooooooooom!

POETS' CORNER

Samuel Taylor Coleridge wrote to a friend with this story of life at Cambridge, where he was reading Divinity at Jesus, in 1792:

> A party of us had been drinking wine together, and three or four freshmen were most deplorably intoxicated – (I have too

great a respect for delicacy to say Drunk). As we were returning homewards two of them fell into the gutter. We ran to assist one of them – who very generously stuttered out, as he lay sprawling in the mud – Nn no nn no! – ssave my ffrfrfriend there – never mind me – *I* can swim.

SMOOTH LITTLE RUNNER

Lord (Jeffrey) Archer in his heyday as a Tory grandee was familiar in London's traffic jams from behind the wheel of his red Mini. The car had been built to his own specification, colour included. Why not Conservative blue, he was forever being asked.

'It isn't red,' he would invariably reply. 'It is claret.'

GOOD COMPANION

As a rule, wine producers know better than to test the expertise of their critics. But Alistair Robertson, when he was chairman of the grand old port shippers Taylor, Fladgate and Yeatman, could not resist setting a tasting test to the party of writers with whom I visited the lodges in Vila Nova de Gaia back in the 1990s. We were each given several glasses of port. They included a simple 'ruby', a late-bottled vintage, a good single quinta wine of recent date, and a grand, mature and frightfully expensive vintage port. Which, Alistair asked us, with an air of breezy confidence in our certain knowledge, was which?

In spite of the fact that our group included a renowned British wine merchant, the correspondents of two national newspapers and the editor of a leading wine magazine, none among us got them all correct. The two of us who came off worst were the humorous writer Auberon Waugh and myself. He got only one right, and I none. 'You,' said Bron to me with warmth, 'are just the sort of person I like to travel with.'

PURPLE PROSE I

'An athletic wine of great refinement, a wine with the muscular strength not of a weightlifter but of a ballet dancer, a Nureyev.' Hubrecht Duijker on Château Maucaillou of Moulis, Bordeaux in *The Good Wines of Bordeaux* (Mitchell Beazley, 1983).

PURPLE PROSE II

Good estates named Prum abound along the sedate Mosel River, but only Joh. Jos. Prum belonged both to Germany's and the world's winemaking elite. The owner, Dr Manfred Prum, is synonymous with individualistic, chromatic, long-lived rieslings that scintillate, no matter their price and age. To taste whites with him in his patrician manor house, a land-mark in Bernkastel-Wehlen, is to find yourself in a Thomas Mann novel. Mann, in 1951, wrote, 'My endeavor is to make the heavy light.' That ideal precisely describes Dr Prum's lithe 1996 riesling kabinett, which opens with a honeysuckle bouquet and segues into a tangy burst of flavor that is part orange-marmalade reduction, part peaches and part marzipan, all dancing to a tiny spritz.

Howard Goldberg in *New York Times*, 6 June 1999

WAUGH (THE OTHER ONE) ON WINE

Evelyn Waugh wrote articles and books about wine, and managed to insinuate the topic into his novels, including some much-admired passages in *Brideshead Revisited*. But it has long been rumoured that he lacked any real appreciation of wine himself. Like many of his contemporaries from relatively humble backgrounds, Waugh knew nothing until arriving at Oxford where, in the 1920s, much in the way of *Brideshead*'s narrator Charles Ryder, he set about climbing the social ladder. This called for an acquaintance with wine, a curricular subject for upper-crust undergraduates as well as the dons. Waugh, it appears, remained below the salt. His loathed history tutor at Hertford College, C.R.M.F. Cruttwell, recalled Waugh with comprehensive contempt. He was, he said, 'a silly little suburban sod with an inferiority complex and no palate'.

TERMS OF ENDEARMENT

At lunch with the regal City of London wine merchants Corney & Barrow I was lucky enough to be seated next to the beautiful writer and broadcaster Victoria Mather. A magnum of Château Léoville Barton of venerable vintage had been served, and we were all listening to another guest, the renowned expert Clive Coates, pronouncing at length how poor it was. For myself, I liked the wine, and asked my neighbour, *sotto voce*, what did she make of it? Ms Mather took a sip and regarded me levelly: 'I think it's absolutely whizzo,' she whispered.

Who could have put it better?

Louis Trebuchet is a leading *négociant* in Burgundy and former president of the region's wine trade association. On the occasion I met him at his headquarters in Puligny-Montrachet, he had just seen a private customer, a wealthy Texan who had come with his glamorous wife to taste the new wines. The gorgeously coiffed consort had tried the Bâtard-Montrachet and declared, 'Now *that* makes my ass *sparkle!*'

Through the tears of laughter, Trebuchet said his only regret was that so few of his customers were prepared to be so exquisitely expressive of their feelings about his wines.

DRY VERSIFIER

The *Rubaiyat of Omar Khayyam*, the work of a lyrically inclined eleventh-century Persian mathematician, is among the most alluring hymns to wine drinking. So it has always seemed odd that the scholarly poet Edward Fitzgerald, who made the *Rubaiyat* immortal with his English translation of 1859, was a teetotaller, and a vegetarian to boot.

IN CASE OF HEADACHE

At a 2009 press tasting of wines from the excellent range offered by the Co-op, Anthony Rose, of *The Independent*, asked me rather gleefully if I had noticed the name emblazoned on the sponsored pens kindly supplied to us for making our notes. It was Panadol.

BRAHMS AND LIST

Johannes Brahms (1833–97) was serious about wine, and his habit in restaurants was simply to demand the best wine available. In one Vienna establishment, the sommelier presented the bottle with toadying assurances to the great composer that it was, 'if you will permit me to say so, sir, a veritable Brahms of a wine'.

'In that case,' Brahms told him, 'take it away, and bring me a Mozart.'

TOUJOURS LA POLITESSE

Tom Innes, who quit his career as a Middle Temple barrister to open a wine business in Monmouth called Fingal Rock, imports mainly from France. He visits the vineyards every winter to meet the growers. After the difficult 2008 harvest and in the midst of the terrible economic downturn, he found some of the *vignerons* not quite their usual selves.

Before his trip, Tom was ringing around to make appointments.

He rang one grower in the Loire, with whom he had been dealing for years, and the conversation went something like this:

> Tom: 'Je suis Tom Innes du Pays de Galles.'
> Grower: 'Bonjour.'
> Tom: 'Comment allez-vous?'
> Grower: [rather gruffly] 'Hein?'
> Tom: 'Comment allez-vous?'
> Grower: [even more gruffly] 'Hein?'
> Tom: 'Well, I was just asking how you were.'
> Grower: 'Pourquoi? Vous êtes docteur?'
> Tom: 'Oh, dear . . .'

Tom tried again to explain that he was Tom Innes, that he'd been buying wine from the grower for several years, and that he hoped to come and buy some more. Suddenly, the tone changed: 'Toutes mes excuses!' The grower hadn't realized who it was – he thought Tom was from a foreign call centre. Two weeks later at the domaine, he was still apologizing. According to Tom, though, his new wines were very good and more than made up for his error.

MY FAVOURITE WINE JOKE

Restaurant customer to wine waiter: 'Do you have a Mâcon?'
  Wine waiter: 'No, monsieur. This is the uniform of a sommelier.'

PUT OUT

A reminiscence from the peripatetic Michael Palin on one of his

Far Eastern television tours: 'Near the Vietnamese border I had to drink wine out of a buffalo horn as part of a local ceremony,' he recalls in *Mentelle Notes*, newsletter of Antipodean wine company Cape Mentelle. 'It was strong and unremarkable, but the winespeak was spot on. "We save this," said my translator, peering into my glazed eyes, "for our most extinguished guests."'

THE LAST WORD

Sign in Bath wine merchant's shop: CLOSING DOWN. COME IN AND PICK OVER OUR OLD BEAUNES.

The ultimate readers' guide to the works that fooled publishers, readers and critics the world over

When Dionysius the Renegade faked a Sophocles text in 400BC to humiliate an academic rival, he paved the way for two millennia of increasingly outlandish literary hoaxers. The path from his mischievous stunt to more serious tricksters takes in every sort of writer: from the religious zealot to the bored student.

For the first time, the complete history of this fascinating sub-genre of world literature is revealed.

Melissa Katsoulis is a journalist and writer. She has written for *The Times*, the *Sunday Telegraph* and the *Financial Times*. She lives in London.

September 2009
Paperback £8.99
978-1-84901-080-1

www.constablerobinson.com

**The captivating and amusing account of the twenty-five books
that have influenced the life of bibliophile Rick Gekoski**

'Think Bill Bryson, only on books' *Tatler*

Outside of a Dog is the captivating account of twenty-five books
drawn from the fields of literature, psychology and philosophy,
and a memoir of a reading self.

Tracing the formative role that books have played in his life,
Rick Gekoski trains the same ironic and analytic eye on these books
and their authors as he does on himself. The result is unique:
a sustained, witty book dedicated to the proposition that
we are what we read. The resulting selection ranges from
Descartes and Freud to works by W.B. Yeats, T.S. Eliot,
and even Roald Dahl.

August 2009
Hardback £14.99
978-1-84529-883-8

www.constablerobinson.com